£2.50

F

The Bridge is Love

Refugee
by
Naomi Blake ARBS
(*See page 40*)

THE BRIDGE IS LOVE

An Anthology of Hope

Collected by
Elizabeth Basset

Foreword by
Sir John Betjeman CBE
Poet Laureate

Darton, Longman and Todd
London

First published in 1981 by
Darton, Longman and Todd Ltd
89 Lillie Road
London SW6 1UD

ISBN 0 232 51541 7

All royalties earned by the sale of this book are being given to 'The Golden Book of the Invalid Children's Aid Society'

British Library Cataloguing in Publication Data

The Bridge of love.
1. Devotional literature
I. Basset, Elizabeth
242 BV4085

ISBN 0–232–51541–7

Typeset by Input Typesetting Ltd., London SW19 8DR
Printed in Great Britain by The Anchor Press Ltd
and Wm Brendon & Son Ltd
both of Tiptree, Essex

To Bryan and Carey

As a meteor glides silent for a moment among the fixed stars and is gone—so among the words of this book glides eluding that other Word which reveals their significance; wonderful, eternal—when these words perish and fall apart from each other that word shall not perish but return thither whence it sprang.

(*Towards Democracy*, Edward Carpenter)

Contents

Foreword ix

Preface xi

PART I

Creation 3

Wonder 15

Longing 31

PART II

Living 45

Loving 64

Laughter and Joy 76

PART III

Looking and Listening 89

The Artist 98

The Dancer 103

The Sculptor 109

The Musician 116

The Poet 124

PART IV

Praying 137

Dreaming 149

Dying 156

Index of Sources and Acknowledgements 171

Foreword

You will want to keep this book on a bedside table. Look at the Contents List, every facet of life is covered. It is positive and encouraging. It is what an Anthology should be, an essential corrective to gloom.

Years of reading and quiet have gone to its making, may it spread like ripples in a still pool.

SIR JOHN BETJEMAN

Preface

This is an anthology of other men's insights and inspirations. I think predominantly it is about awareness—awareness of that other dimension, that mystery which makes the living of every day infinitely exciting and worth while: an awareness, a perception, an openness, a receptiveness to that which can really only be seen or heard or understood in the still, silent centre of our souls, but which is conveyed by all the sights and sounds, the joys and sorrows of our daily living. It is full of hope, even in the darkest days of suffering and anxiety, and the bridge to it is love, the bridge of communication between people, the bridge of communication supremely between the Creator and his creation: the awareness of Love.

'What is it that makes your heart sing?' This question is sometimes asked by a counsellor of someone he is meeting for the first time. In this book the reader will find the answer—given by the poet, the musician, the artist, the sculptor and the ordinary man in his need to create, and I believe the answer at the deepest level is always the same.

It is impossible for me to thank by name all those who have helped me, but I hope that the book itself will be my way of thanking them. I would also like to record my gratitude to all the writers whose words I have quoted for sharing their insights and inspirations with us.

I would like to say 'thank you' most of all to Sir John Betjeman, not only for so kindly agreeing to write the foreword for this collection, but also for all the encouragement he has given me. But for him, my first anthology, *Love is My Meaning*, would never have been published. I shall never cease to be grateful to him for his 'awareness'.

Elizabeth Basset
London 1981

Part I

CREATION

WONDER

LONGING

CREATION

'And God saw that the light was good'

Genesis 1:1, The Common Bible

In the beginning God created the heavens and the earth. The earth was without form and void, and darkness was upon the face of the deep; and the Spirit of God was moving over the face of the waters. And God said, 'Let there be light' and there was light, and God saw that the light was good.

From **For All Mankind** *by* Stuart Blanch

The book of Genesis fills me with great hope, when hope is in short supply. It fills me with great hope because one great man of God, the author of this book, looking back across the wrecks of time, haunted by his own inadequacies, bored by the brutalities and banalities of everyday existence, still holds fast to paradise.

It must be so if the Lord is Lord of all.

By Metropolitan Philaret of Moscow, *quoted in* **The Orthodox Way** *by* Kallistos Ware

All creatures are balanced upon the creative word of God, as if upon a bridge of diamond; above them is the abyss of divine infinitude, below them that of their own nothingness.

From **Enfolded In Love** *by* Julian of Norwich

See I Am God.
God is the still point at the centre.
There is no doer but he.

All this he showed me with great joy, saying, 'See, I am God. See I am in all things. See I do all things. See I never take my hands off my work, nor ever shall, through all eternity. See I lead all things to the end I have prepared for them. I do this by the same wisdom and love and power through which I made them. How can anything be done that is not well done?

God wants us to know that he keeps us safe through good and ill.

We shall see God face to face, simply and wholly.

From **Markings** *by* Dag Hammarskjöld

So shall the world be created each morning anew, *forgiven*—in Thee, by Thee.

Anonymous, *quoted by* St Thomas Aquinas *in* **Catena Aurea**

THE CRUCIFIXION

God withdrew the protection but did not break the union.

Isaiah 35, The Jerusalem Bible

Let the wilderness and the dry-lands exult,
let the wasteland rejoice and bloom,
let it bring forth flowers like the jonquil,
let it rejoice and sing for joy.

The glory of Lebanon is bestowed on it,
the splendour of Carmel and Sharon;
they shall see the glory of Yahweh,
the splendour of our God.

Strengthen all weary hands,
steady all trembling knees
and say to all faint hearts,
'Courage!'. Do not be afraid.

'Look, your God is coming,
vengeance is coming,
the retribution of God;
he is coming to save you.'

Then the eyes of the blind shall be opened,
the ears of the deaf unsealed,
then the lame shall leap like a deer
and the tongues of the dumb sing for joy;

for water gushes in the desert,
streams in the wasteland,
the scorched earth becomes a lake,
the parched land springs of water.

The lairs where the jackals used to live
become thickets of reed and papyrus . . .

And through it will run a highway undefiled
which shall be called the Sacred Way;
the unclean may not travel by it,
nor fools stray along it.

No lion will be there
nor any fierce beast roam about it,
but the redeemed will walk there,
for those Yahweh has ransomed shall return.

They will come to Zion shouting for joy,
everlasting joy on their faces;
joy and gladness will go with them
and sorrow and lament be ended.

To Be a Christian *by* Dietrich Bonhoeffer

To be a Christian does not mean to be religious in a particular way but to be a man—not a type of man but the man Christ creates in us.

From **Collected Poems**
by Edna St Vincent Millay

GOD'S WORLD

O world, I cannot hold thee close enough!
Thy winds, thy wide grey skies!
Thy mists, that roll and rise!
Thy woods, this autumn day, that ache and sag
And all but cry with color! That gaunt crag
To crush! To lift the lean of that black bluff!
World, World, I cannot get thee close enough!

Long have I known a glory in it all,
But never knew I this;
Here such a passion is
As stretcheth me apart, Lord, I do fear
Thou'st made the world too beautiful this year;
My soul is all but out of me,—let fall
No burning leaf; prithee, let no bird call.

From **Gitanjali** *by* Rabindranath Tagore

LIX

Yes, I know, this is nothing but thy love, O beloved of my heart—this golden light that dances upon the leaves, these idle clouds sailing across the sky, this passing breeze leaving its coolness upon my forehead.

The morning light has flooded my eyes—this is thy message to my heart. Thy face is bent from above, thy eyes look down on my eyes, and my heart has touched thy feet.

From **Love's Endeavour, Love's Expense** *by*
W. H. Vanstone

A HYMN TO THE CREATOR

Morning glory, starlit sky,
Leaves in springtime, swallows' flight,
Autumn gales, tremendous seas,
Sounds and scents of summer night;

Soaring music, tow'ring words,
Art's perfection, scholar's truth,
Joy supreme of human love,
Memory's treasure, grace of youth;

Open, Lord, are these, Thy gifts,
Gifts of love to mind and sense;
Hidden is love's agony,
Love's endeavour, love's expense.

Love that gives gives ever more,
Gives with zeal, with eager hands,
Spares not, keeps not, all outpours,
Ventures all, its all expends.

Drained is love in making full;
Bound in setting others free;
Poor in making many rich;
Weak in giving power to be.

Therefore He Who Thee reveals
Hangs, O Father, on that Tree
Helpless; and the nails and thorns
Tell of what Thy love must be.

Thou art God; no monarch Thou
Thron'd in easy state to reign;
Thou art God, Whose arms of love
Aching, spent, the world sustain.

From **Adonais** *by* P. B. Shelley

XVIII

Ah, woe is me! Winter is come and gone,
But grief returns with the revolving year;
The airs and streams renew their joyous tone;
The ants, the bees, the swallows reappear;
Fresh leaves and flowers deck the dead Seasons' bier;
The amorous birds now pair in every brake,
And build their mossy homes in field and brere;
And the green lizard, and the golden snake,
Like unimprisoned flames, out of their trance awake.

XIX

Through wood and stream and field and hill and Ocean
A quickening life from the Earth's heart has burst
As it has ever done, with change and motion,
From the great morning of the world when first
God dawned on Chaos; in its stream immersed,
The lamps of Heaven flash with a softer light;
All baser things pant with life's sacred thirst;
Diffuse themselves; and spend in love's delight
The beauty and the joy of their renewed might.

Of Gardens *by* Francis Bacon

And because the breath of Flowers is far sweeter in the air (where it comes and goes like the warbling of Musick) than in the hand, therefore nothing is more fit for that delight than to know what be the flowers and plants that do best perfume the air. Roses, damask and red, are fast flowers of their smells; so that you may walk by a whole row of them, and find nothing of their sweetness; yea, though it be in a morning's dew. Bays likewise yield no smell as they grow, Rosemary little, nor Sweet Marjoram; that which above all others yields the sweetest smell in the air is the Violet, especially the White double Violet, which comes twice a year, about the middle of *April* and about *Bartholomew-tide*. Next to that is the Muskrose; then the Strawberry-leaves dying with a most excellent cordial smell, then the flower of the Vines, it is a little dust like the dust of a Bent, which grows upon the cluster in the first coming forth; the Sweet-Briar, then Wallflowers, which are very delightful to be set under a parlour or lower chamber window; then Pinks and Gilliflowers, especially the matted pink, and Clove Gilliflower; then the flowers of the Lime-tree; then the Honey-suckles, so they be somewhat afar off. Of Bean-Flowers I speak not, because they are field-Flowers; but those which perfume the air most delightfully, not passed by as the rest, but being trodden upon and crushed, are three; that is, Burnet, Wild Thyme, and Water Mints; therefore you are to set whole alleys of them, to have the pleasure when you walk or tread.

From **The Complete Poems** *by* Walter de la Mare

THE SNOWDROP

Now—now, as low I stooped, thought I,
I will see what this snowdrop is;
So shall I put much argument by,
And solve a lifetime's mysteries.

A northern wind had frozen the grass;
Its blades were hoar with crystal rime,
Aglint like light-dissecting glass
At beam of morning-prime.

From hidden bulb the flower reared up
Its angled, slender, cold, dark stem,
Whence dangled an inverted cup
For tri-leaved diadem.

Beneath these ice-pure sepals lay
A triplet of green-pencilled snow,
Which in the chill-aired gloom of day
Stirred softly to and fro.

Mind fixed, but else made vacant, I,
Lost to my body, called my soul
To don that frail solemnity,
Its inmost self my goal.

And though in vain—no mortal mind
Across that threshold yet hath fared!—
In this collusion I divined
Some consciousness we shared.

Strange roads—while suns, a myriad, set—
Had led us through infinity;
And where they crossed, there then had met
Not two of us, but three.

Though the days are dark and our hearts fearful, though our anxieties are great for all those we love and we find it hard to trust and be thankful, the beauty of the world we live in surely holds and gives out such a message of hope, spring after winter, light after dark, happiness after sorrow, birth after life.

A fifteenth-century Irish poet, Tadhg Óg Ó hUiggin, *put it so well, I think:*

It is Thou who makest the sun bright, together with the ice; it is Thou who createdst the rivers and the salmon all along the river.

That the nut-tree should be flowering, O Christ, it is a rare craft: through Thy skill too comes the kernel, Thou fair ear of our wheat.

Though the children of Eve ill deserve the bird-flocks and the salmon, it was the Immortal One on the cross who made both the salmon and the birds.

It is He who makes the flower of the sloe grow through the bark of the blackthorn, and the nut-flower on other trees; beside this what miracle is greater?

George Herbert *also bears witness to the fact that God alone is the source of all creative art.*

O Sacred Providence, who from end to end
Strongly and sweetly movest! shall I write
And not of thee, through whom my fingers bend
To hold my quill? shall they not do thee right?

Of all thy creatures both in sea and land
Only to man thou hast made known thy wayes
And put the penne alone into his hand
And made him Secretarie of thy praise. . . .

. . . All things that are, though they have sev'ral wayes
Yet in their being joyn with one advise
To honour thee; and so I give thee praise
In all my other hymnes, but in this twice.

And Helen Keller *in her blindness and deafness:*

I believe that God is in me as the sun is in the colour and fragrance of a flower, the Light in my darkness, the Voice in my silence.

Thomas Merton *affirms the truth of the presence of God in the depths of the soul of each one of us.*

At the centre of our being is a point of nothingness which is untouched by sin and by illusion, a point of pure truth, a point or spark which belongs entirely to God, which is never at our disposal, from which God disposes of our lives, which is inaccessible to the fantasies of our own mind or the brutalities of our own will. This little point of nothingness and of absolute poverty is the pure glory of God in us. It is, so to speak his name written in us, as our poverty, as our indigence, as our dependence, as our sonship. It is like a pure diamond, blazing with the invisible light of heaven. It is in everybody, and if we could see it we would see these billions of points of light coming together in the face and blaze of the sun that would make all the darkness and cruelty of life vanish completely . . . The gate of heaven is everywhere.

From the **Confessions** *of* St Augustine

Wonderful is the depth of Thy words, whose surface see, is before us, gently leading on the little ones; and yet a wonderful deepness, O my God a wonderful deepness. It is awe to look into it; even an awfulness of honour, and a trembling of love.

By Joseph Plunkett, *quoted in* **A Tent in Which to Pass a Summer's Night** *by* Belle Valerie Gaunt *and* George Trevelyan

I see His blood upon the rose
  And in the stars the glory of His eyes
His body gleams amid the eternal snows
  His tears fall from the skies.

I see His face in every flower
  The thunder and the singing of the birds
Are but His voice, and carven by His power
  Rocks are His written words.

All pathways by His feet are worn
  His strong heart stirs the ever-beating sea
His crown of thorns is twined with every thorn
  His cross is every tree.

From **Intimations of Christianity** *by* Simone Weil

The Christ is that key which locks together the Creator and creation. Since knowledge is the reflection of being, the Christ is also by that same token, the key of knowledge. 'Woe unto you, lawyers!' said he, 'for ye have taken away the key of knowledge.' He was that key, He whom earlier centuries had loved in advance, and whom the Pharisees had denied and were going to put to death.

From **Joys And Sorrows: Reflections** *by* Pablo Casals

Sometimes I look about me with a feeling of complete dismay. In the confusion that afflicts the world today, I see a disrespect for the very values of life. Beauty is all about us, but how many are blind to it! They look at the wonder of this earth—and seem to see nothing. People move hectically but give little thought to where they are going. They seek excitement for its mere sake, as if they were lost and desperate. They take little pleasure in the natural and quiet and simple things of life.

Each second we live is a new and unique moment of the universe, a moment that never was before and will never be again.

And what do we teach our children in School? We teach them that two and two make four, and that Paris is in France. When will we also teach them what they are? We should say to each one of them, Do you know what you are? You are a marvel. You are unique. In all the world there is no other child exactly like you. And look at your body—what a wonder it is! Your legs, your arms, your cunning fingers, the way you move. You may become a Shakespeare, a Michelangelo, a Beethoven. You have the capacity for anything. Yes, you are a marvel. When you grow up can you then harm another who is like you, a marvel? You must cherish one another. You must work, we all must work—to make the world worthy of its children . . .

The love of one's country is a natural thing. But why should love stop at the border? Our Family is one—each of us has a duty to his brothers. We are all leaves of a tree, and that tree is humanity.

From **Enfolded in Love** *by* Julian of Norwich

I saw, that all compassion to one's fellow Christians, exercised in love, is a mark of Christ's indwelling.

From an article by Gerald Priestland *in* **Common Ground**

TO WHAT CAN WE WITNESS TOGETHER?

For many years I have been convinced that before one man can hit another with intent to destroy him, it is necessary for him to regard his victim as lower than—other than—himself: as not being a fellow human at all, but some lower species of animal. If we could see the man we bomb or bayonet as our brother, we could not destroy him, and to see him as anything else is again the blasphemy against the Fatherhood of God. Jews know that better than anyone, for they have been the constant victims of the lie that they are less than human, other than the rest of us.

We, in this community, are better placed than most Christians to denounce that, to bear witness in our behaviour as well as our words that it is not so.

• • •

I'm still amazed how often I have to remind people, that Jesus was a Jew—a non-conformist and even heretical Jew, maybe, but one whose every other word is to be traced back to Jewish religious literature. He died with a Psalm on his lips—not the Thirty Nine Articles, the Nicene Creed or the Westminster Confession—and Christians are too ready to forget how much of what they sing, read and recite in their services bears witness to the sprituality of Jewry.

From **Selected Poems** *by* Mervyn Peake

TO MAEVE

You walk unaware
Of the slender gazelle
That moves as you move
And is one with the limbs
That you have.

You live unaware
Of the faint, the unearthly
Echo of hooves
That within your white streams
Of clear clay that I love,

Are in flight as you turn,
As you stand, as you move,
As you sleep, for the slender
Gazelle never rests
In your ivory grove.

WONDER

'Saved by wonder'

From **The Universe and Dr. Einstein** *by* Albert Einstein

The most beautiful and most profound emotion we can experience is the sensation of the mystical. It is the source of all true science. He to whom this emotion is a stranger, who can no longer wonder and stand rapt in awe, is as good as dead.

To know that what is impenetrable to us really exists manifesting itself as the highest wisdom and the most radiant beauty which our dull faculties can comprehend only in their most primitive forms—this knowledge, this feeling is at the centre of true religiousness.

From **Markings** *by* Dag Hammarskjöld

The 'mystical experience'. Always *here* and *now*—in that freedom which is one with distance in that stillness which is born of silence. But—this is a freedom in the midst of action, a stillness in the midst of other human beings. The mystery is a constant reality to him who, in this world, is free from self-concern, a reality that grows peaceful and mature before the receptive attention of assent.

In our era the road to holiness necessarily passes through the world of action.

By Oliver Wendell Holmes: **The English Hymnal** no. 434

AWE

Lord of all being, throned afar,
Thy glory flames from sun and star;
Centre and soul of every sphere,
Yet to each loving heart how near!

Sun of our life, Thy quickening ray
Sheds on our path the glow of day;
Star of our hope, Thy softened light
Cheers the long watches of the night.

Our midnight is thy smile withdrawn,
Our noontide is thy gracious dawn,
Our rainbow arch thy mercy's sign;
All, save the clouds of sin, are thine.

Lord of all life, below, above,
Whose light is truth, whose warmth is love,
Before Thy ever-blazing throne
We ask no lustre of our own.

Grant us thy truth to make us free
And kindling hearts that burn for thee,
Till all Thy living altars claim
One holy light, one heavenly flame.

From **A Pool of Reflections** *by* Raynor Johnson

No aspiring soul, has not at some time bowed in worship before the wonder, mystery and beauty of this world. The glorious forms and colours of sunset and dawn; the ripple of moonlight on the surface of some quiet lake; the majesty of mountain peaks; and the quaintly flowing music of mountain streams, remind every lover of Nature that God is not apart from His world, but can be found hidden there as the very Spirit of it all—'Beauty Itself among beautiful things'. The beauty is there for all to see, but men dwell in the shadows of their own creation and their eyes are blind to it. We miss the joy of the beautiful so often, because we are wrapped up in ourselves.

From **Becoming What I Am** *by* H. A. Williams

St Augustine uses the word memory, *memoria*, to describe not what we remember in the ordinary sense, but all the experiences, impressions and ideas which have impinged upon us and which are now stored somewhere within us even though in the ordinary sense we have forgotten most of them. By memory St Augustine meant something very like what today we call the unconscious. And the most important part of us which is fed by what we read is our unconscious minds. Ideas impinge upon us as we read and we then apparently forget them, or most of them. But we didn't therefore lose them. They remain with us in what St Augustine called our memory. They thus help to make us what we are, and to repeat it again, it is by means of what we are that God works within us.

From **The Initials in the Heart** *by* Laurence Whistler

Do you know that half-comprehension of some immense truth? It sparks in a corner of the mind that you're not looking at—when you look it's gone. The words 'intimations of immortality' mean that to me.

By St Symeon (949–1022), *quoted in* **The Orthodox Way** *by* Kallistos Ware

It is invisible, and no hand can lay hold of it;
Intangible, and yet it can be felt everywhere. . . .
What is it? O wonder! What is it not? For it has no name.
In my foolishness I tried to grasp it,
And I closed my hand, thinking that I held it fast:
But it escaped, and I could not retain it in my fingers.
Full of sadness, I unclenched my grip
And I saw it once again in the palm of my hand.
O unutterable wonder! O strange mystery!
Why do we trouble ourselves in vain? Why do we all wander astray?

From **A Rumour of Angels** *by* Peter L. Berger

A rediscovery of the supernatural will be, above all a regaining of openness in our perception of reality. It will not only be, as theologians influenced by existentialism have greatly over-emphasized, an overcoming of tragedy. Perhaps more importantly it will be an overcoming of triviality. In openness to the signals of transcendence the true proportions of our experience are rediscovered. This is the comic relief of redemption; it makes it possible for us to laugh and to play with a new fulness.

From **The Savage and Beautiful Country** *by* Alan McGlashan

REMEMBERING AND FORGETTING

What is needed is an extension of contemporary consciousness to include what can be defined as the translucent quality in all things; the quality by which an object or an event is seen not only as a thing-in-itself, but also as a membrane through which can dimly be discerned the foetal stirring of a different order of experience.

This once caught, even for a moment, transforms the sensible universe, investing all objects with a sharp intensity of being. . . . The quality of translucence is the key, a golden key that is the careless plaything of all children, and the conscious instrument of a few geniuses. In exceptional moments of their lives ordinary men and women may fleetingly hold it: in the first days of overwhelming love, in the final moments of overwhelming peril, in the presence of new life, and sometimes on the unheralded news of death.

At such moments a man stands on tiptoe, and may catch a startled glimpse of another level of being where all values are changed and everything is understood differently; the level of which Chekov dreamed where 'everything is forgiven, and it would be strange not to forgive.'

. . . To become aware of this translucent quality in all things is no vague romantic goal. . . . It is the basis of all true science, the essence of ritual, the constant attribute of wisdom. It may be the nearest that human minds can reach to the meaning of meaning.

From **The Go-Between God** *by* John V. Taylor

Just when we are safest there's a sunset touch,
A fancy from a flower bell, someone's death,
A chorus ending from Euripedes,
And that's enough for fifty hopes and fears,
As old and new at once as nature's self,
To rap and knock and enter in our soul.
Robert Browning

Now if it is these moments of recognition and awareness that change our minds and change our lives, if these can be the true turning points of human history, then something of enormous power must be at work in such commonplace experiences. One might say that a flash of recognition has a higher voltage than a flash of lightning, that the power that makes us suddenly aware is the secret of all evolution and the spark that sets off most revolutions.

But what is this force which causes me to see in a way in which I have not seen? What makes a landscape or a person or an idea come to life for me and become a presence towards which I surrender myself? I recognize, I respond, I fall in love, I worship—yet it was not I who took the first step. In every such encounter there has been an anonymous third party who makes the introduction, acts as a go-between, makes two beings aware of each other, sets up a current of communication between them. What is more, this invisible go-between does not simply stand between us but is activating us from inside, Moses approaching the burning bush is no scientific observer; the same fiery essence burns in his own heart also. He and the thorn-bush are caught and held, as it were, in the same magnetic field.

From **Equus** *by* Peter Shaffer

What worship has *he* ever known? Real worship! Without worship you shrink, it's as brutal as that . . . I shrank my *own* life.

From **Cardinal Newman** *by* J. Lewis May

And yet in spite of the universal world which we see, there is another world, quite as far spreading, quite as close to us and more wonderful; another world all around us, though we see it not, and more wonderful than the world we see, for this reason if for no other, that we do not see it. All around us are numberless objects coming and going, watching, working or waiting, which we see not: this is that other world which the eyes reach not unto, but faith only.

From **The Go-Between God** *by* John V. Taylor

It is not more wonders that we need but more Wonder.

From **Truth: A Path and Not a Possession,** *Swarthmore Lecture 1977 by* Damaris Parker-Rhodes

The spirit has its own senses by which to see, feel and be guided; these grow out of our ordinary ones and are related to them, as inward eyes, ears and feelings, which as yet are only partly formed and rudimentary, but which develop as we dare to trust them. Mystical experience and knowledge of guidance are becoming commoner in these times and perhaps this is because the great Unseen is building up power to help us in these dark days.

At last we are ready on a great scale to begin to understand what is happening in the polarization of old and new. I believe it will not be too many years ahead before we begin to educate children in a fuller use of their mind's and spirit's potential . . . This way is open to everyone; the seed of divine consciousness of which Christ's incarnation is the herald is not out in space but here, right under our hands to be experienced in fulness of life as we learn to look for it: as we dig in the garden, sit by the bedside of the dying, hold a young baby in our arms, study the patterns of nature through microscope and telescope, puzzle over philosophical problems and above all as we sit in the silence both alone and together in the meeting for worship.

From **The Garden** *by* Victoria Sackville-West

Small is our vision, rare the searchlight beam
Few moments given, but in truth supreme
Transcendent moments, when the simpler theme
Is suddenly perceived
And by our intricate uncertainty
We are no more deceived.

From **Markings** *by* Dag Hammarskjöld

The light died in the low clouds. Falling snow drank in the dusk. Shrouded in silence, the branches wrapped me in their peace. When the boundaries were erased, once again the wonder: that *I* exist.

By Raymond Queneau, *quoted in* **Jesus Ahead** *by* Gerard Bessiere

POEM

When alive in its shell
the mollusc never spoke
easily to man.
Now it is dead it tells
the whole sea into the child's ear
and the child is amazed.

From **Prometheus Unbound** *by* P. B. Shelley

Ione: Thou most desired Hour, more loved and lovely
Than all thy sisters, this is the mystic shell;
See the pale azure fading into silver
Lining it with soft yet glowing light:
Looks it not like lulled music sleeping there?
Spirit: It seems in truth the fairest shell of Ocean:
Its sound must be at once both sweet and strange.

From **In Tune With the Infinite** *by* Ralph Waldo Trine

Let there be many windows in your soul,
That all the glory of the universe,
May beautify it. Not the narrow pane
Of one poor creed can catch the radiant rays
That shine from countless sources. Tear away
The blinds of superstition; let the light
Pour through fair windows, broad as truth itself
And high as heaven . . . Tune your ear
To all the worldless music of the stars
And to the voice of nature, and your heart
Shall turn to truth and goodness as the plant
Turns to the sun. A thousand unseen hands
Reach down to help you to their peace-crowned heights,
And all the forces of the firmament
Shall fortify your strength. Be not afraid
To thrust aside half-truths and grasp the whole.

From **Return to the Centre** *by* Bede Griffiths

As the Upanishad says:

'There is a space within the heart in which all space is contained. Both heaven and earth are contained within it, both fire and air, both sun and moon, both lightning and stars.

. . . And there all things are found as they exist eternally in the Word, of which it is said, "That which has been made was life in him" . . . . It is the Spirit in man which first gives us life—the Lord God "breathed into his nostrils the breath of life"; and man became a living being and this awakens consciousness in us.'

From **Poems** *by* Gerard Manley Hopkins

GOD'S GRANDEUR

The world is charged with the grandeur of God.
  It will flame out, like shining from shook foil;
  It gathers to a greatness, like the ooze of oil
Crushed. Why do men then now not reck his rod?
Generations have trod, have trod, have trod;

And all is seared with trade; bleared, smeared with toil;
And wears man's smudge and shares man's smell: the soil
Is bare now, nor can foot feel, being shod.

And for all this, nature is never spent;
There lives the dearest freshness deep down things;
And though the last lights off the black west went
Oh, morning, at the brown brink eastward, springs—
Because the Holy Ghost over the bent
World broods with warm breast and with ah! bright wings.

Anonymous, probably Japanese

He was a man who understood the 'ah' in things.

Space *by* E.B.

Space to breathe, space to grow, space to listen and to look, space to pray, space to *be*. *Space*.

Though of itself it holds nothing, it at the same time holds everything together.

It is impossible to think of anything which has life or meaning which does not owe its very existence to the space within which it is contained. Without space to breathe all life withers and dies.

In the arts it is perhaps in sculpture that the value of space (the holes between) is most obvious. But music, dancing, painting, singing and writing all also depend upon the 'apartness' of space for their full beauty to be realized.

Who has not been daunted by the too closely written page, or by the wall too full of paintings?

In prayer and meditation the words used gain meaning and potency when interspersed with silence. Sometimes we yearn for a few silent moments in church or listening to an address so that we can absorb what has just been said or felt. In poetry especially the spacing is of paramount importance. One could go on for ever, but I think Gerard Manley Hopkins sums it up in the last two lines of his poem 'The Grandeur of God'. If we can put the *ah*! into living then I feel the bright wings cannot help but be there.

From **Bread for the Winter Birds** *By* Thomas Blackburn

THE AUTHORIZED VERSION

Remember the words do
Include the silences
And that some words are
Alive in their pauses
The divine can breathe in.
For themes of the spirit
Need gaps to suggest how
No words quite inherit
Themes that supreme are
So the great words meet
With sound and silence.
They need what is not
Quite said for truth's sake:
And since we're finite
Only the silences
Can suggest infinite
Meetings, humilities.

From a lecture by Claude Curling

Space is for the extension of love.
Time is for the evolution of love.
Matter is for the expression of love.
Eternity is for the living of love.

From an article by A.M. Allchin *in* **Christian**

SOLITUDE AND COMMUNION IN THE LIFE OF THOMAS MERTON

He had the powerful conviction, common to all the great representatives of the tradition of Christian spirituality, that what he was given was not for himself alone, but for all who could and would hear. He was by natural gift a writer, one whose business is with words. He felt all the more acutely the innumerable ways in which words are threatened and destroyed in our society. He knew, too, the healing power of silence, and the necessary dialectic which there is between speech and silence. 'For language to have meaning, there must be intervals of silence somewhere to divide word from word, and utterance from utterance. He who retires into silence does not necessarily hate language. Perhaps it is love and respect for language which impose silence upon him. For the mercy of God is not heard in words unless it is heard, both before and after the words are spoken in silence.' Anyone who has noticed the quality which words receive when spoken out of silence, whether in time of retreat, or in the setting of a monastic community will recognize the truth of this statement. But of course, it has wider and further implications.

. . . 'To be here with the silence of Sonship in my heart is to be a center in which all things converge upon you. This is surely enough for the time being.

'Therefore, Father, I beg you to keep me in this silence so that I may learn from it the word of your peace, and the word of your mercy and the word of your gentleness to the world: and that through me perhaps your word of peace may make itself heard where it has not been possible for anyone to hear it for a long time.

'To study truth here and learn to suffer for truth.

'The light itself, and the contentment and the Spirit, these are enough, Amen.'

From **Prometheus Unbound** *by* P. B. Shelley

Ione: Listen too,
  How every pause is filled with under-notes,
  Clear, silver, icy, keen, awakening tones,
  Which pierce the sense, and live within the soul,
  As the sharp stars pierce winter's crystal air
  And gaze upon themselves within the sea.

From **The Zodiac Arch** *by* Freya Stark

ON SILENCE

A part of all art is to make silence speak. The things left out in painting, the note witheld in music, the void in architecture—all are as necessary and as active as the utterance itself. I have often thought of this in a cathedral, watching the Gothic spaces move into their shadows, or in the mosques of Istanbul, where I would slip my shoes off and turn in for a short rest when the cobbled streets left me exhausted. The so-called New Mosque, with its late but beautiful blue tiles, was near the terminus of my Bosphorus steamer, and I would sit there on my way and watch not the structure but the space it enclosed, in whose dimness the barefoot people touched their foreheads to the ground. In Saint Sophia this beauty of emptiness that has acquired a shape seems to me more visible than that in any other building I know. These things, too, are voices of silence, which is as inseparable from any sort of utterance as a shadow from its sun.

From **Christian Faith and Practice in the Experience of the Religious Society of Friends:** Section 244 *by* Rufus M. Jones

[The early Friends] made the discovery that silence is one of the best preparations for communion [with God] and for the reception of inspiration and guidance. Silence itself, of course has no magic. It may be just sheer emptiness, absence of words or noise or music. It may be an occasion for slumber, or it may be a dead form. But it may be an intensified pause, a vitalised hush, a creative quiet, an actual moment of mutual and reciprocal correspondence with God. The actual meeting of man with God and God with man is the very crown and culmination of what we can do with our human life here on earth.

From **Perseus in the Wind** *by* Freya Stark

Religion is all an adventure in courage, and superstition a print of adventuring footsteps in the past, though it is apt to become more coercive than a footprint and to freeze, if it can, the exploring spirit from which itself was born. That I imagine is why the mystic is inclined to retreat from the habitations of man; to seek a world where every object he sees is not wound in a cocoon of thought and images created by others. He needs to get away from all these voices, he needs a footstool for meditation, and to watch, in the silence of his own heart, for the trail which so many wayfarers have confused. The true call of the desert, of the mountains, or the sea, is their silence—free of the network of dead speech. This silence without which no enduring progress can be built must enter into all education that is worthy of the name: it is the reason why climbing or walking or sailing should come, if possible, into the life of every child:

The thought of death sits easy on the man
Who has been born and dies among the mountains.
Wordsworth, 'The Brothers'

Some people, out of strength or weakness, come to love such solitude as the breath of life. Many, strangers to their own souls, shun it with fear. But the well-strung creature finds in it a tonic, a pause from which he comes refreshed. With the mountain lightness still in his eyes and feet, he is happy to return from the wilderness and to find himself again among the paths and dwellings and habits, the rites and symbols which in their long trail of history have made him what he is.

From **A Gift Of Light** *by* Father Andrew

CONTRAST

I saw the morn break glorious o'er the sea
With all the ritual of its pageantry:
Soft herald lights shone first, then splendidly
Crimson and gold gave welcome royally:
The dim dawn curtains parted, and the sun,
A great gold circle, slowly, solemnly,
Proclaiming that a new day had begun,
Rose from his palace underneath the sea.

From that magnificence I went my way
Down to the village church below the hill,
And there with simple souls I knelt to pray,
With them to learn submission to His will
Who with true poverty could be content;
And as my Lord in mercy came to me
In the small circle of the sacrament,
I marvelled at His deep humility.

From **The Shape of the Liturgy** *by* Dom Gregory Dix

DO THIS IN REMEMBRANCE OF ME

Was ever another command so obeyed?

For century after century, spreading slowly to every continent and country and among every race on earth, this action has been done, in every conceivable human circumstance, for every conceivable human need from infancy and before it to extreme old age and after it, from the pinnacles of earthly greatness to the refuge of fugitives in the caves and dens of the earth. Men have found no better thing than this to do for Kings at their crowning, and for criminals going to the scaffold; for armies in triumph or for a bride and bridegroom in a little country church, for the proclamation of a dogma or for a good crop of wheat; for the wisdom of the Parliament of a mighty nation or for a sick old woman afraid to die, for a schoolboy sitting his examination or for Columbus setting forth to discover America; for the famine of a whole province or for the soul of a dead lover; in thankfulness that my father did not die of pneumonia; for a village headman much tempted to return to fetich because the yams had failed, because the Turk was at the gates of Vienna. For the repentance of Margaret, for the settlement of a strike; for a son for a barren woman, for Captain so-and-so, wounded and a prisoner of war; while the lions roared in the nearby amphitheatre; on the beach at Dunkirk; while the hiss of scythes in the thick June grass came faintly through the windows of the church; tremulously by an old monk on the fiftieth anniversary of his vows, furtively by an exiled bishop who had hewn timber all day in a prison camp near Murmansk; gorgeously, for the canonisation of St. Joan of Arc—one could fill many pages with the reasons why we have done this, and not tell a hundredth part of them. And best of all, week by week, and month by month, on a hundred thousand successive Sundays, faithfully and unfailingly, across all the parishes of Christendom, the pastors have done this just to make the *plebs sancta Dei*—the holy common people of God.

To those who know a little of christian history probably the most moving of all the reflections it brings is not the thought of the great events and well-remembered saints, but of those innumerable millions of entirely obscure faithful men and women every one with his or her own individual hopes and fears and joys and sorrows and loves—and sins and temptations and prayers—once every whit as vivid and alive as mine are now. They have left no slightest trace in the world, not even a name, but have passed to God utterly forgotten by man. Yet each of them once believed and prayed as I believe and pray, and found it hard and grew slack and sinned and repented and fell again. Each of them worshipped at the Eucharist and found their thought wandering and tried again, and felt heavy and unresponsive and yet know—just as really and pathetically as I do these things. . . . The sheer stupendous quantity of the love of God which this ever-repeated action has drawn from the obscure christian multitudes through the centuries is in itself an overwhelming thought (All that going with one to the altar every morning).

From **The English Hymnal** no. 437

Lost in Wonder, Love and Praise.

From **A Gift Of Light** *by* Father Andrew

COMMUNION IN A COUNTRY CHURCH

I brushed the dew-drenched daisies on the lawn,
I passed the silent cattle in the field
And laborers going out to work at dawn
To seek such store as the good earth should yield.
One silver star was set in the pale gold
Like a dropped jewel of the passing night.
A white mist hung over some sleeping fold
Like a gauze curtain in the morning light;
So—past the river and the little street,
The grey old tombs and solemn ancient yews,
Into the Holy Place, Thy Mercy Seat,
Where Thou, the Lord of all, didst not refuse
To give me a sinner that same morn
To hold and keep the Secret of the Dawn.

Prayer *from* All Saints' Church, Margaret Street, London

Come Holy Spirit of God restore the lives which without you are dead.
Kindle the hearts which without you are cold and dull.
Enlighten the minds which without you are dark and blind;
Fill the Church which without you is an empty shrine.
And lead us Lord to pray.

LONGING

'Some of us call it longing
And others call it God'

From **Markings** *by* Dag Hammarskjöld

Something to live for great enough to die for.

By E. B.

Life is a search for this 'something', a search for something or someone to give meaning to our lives, to answer the question, who am I, why am I here, what is the purpose of my life?

I believe that this great need we all feel is caused by a longing which cannot be satisfied by the usual goals we set ourselves in this journey of life. Even when they have been achieved they so often fall short of our hopes and expectations. The longed-for objective is not something which can be possessed, it cannot be held or kept, it can only be fleetingly glimpsed as it comes and goes.

It can only be hinted at, referred to obliquely; indescribable in words, it can only be felt, and all we know of it is that it is what we are longing for. The promise of it is there in our love for another person. In the glory of a sunrise or sunset, the silver path of the moon on the sea, the sad haunting cry of sea-birds, the touching protective courage of a wild thing for its young or its mate. In the mountains and the streams, in the flowers and the forests, in the sufferings and sorrows of mankind as well as in the joys and the laughter.

This longing is all bound up with memories too, it carries its light like a will-o'-the-wisp through the scents and sounds and sights which suddenly bring back to us the magical moments when we were very young and in love with life. But it is also there, playing its part in the despair and the sorrowing and the regrets and the remorse.

Sadly it seems that this yearning can become misdirected into channels which lead to drugs or drink or other excesses for excitement to assuage the longing when it has not been recognized for what it is.

This collection of writings seem to me to demonstrate the countless ways in which the longing can be expressed, by poets and painters, musicians and dancers, and by so many of those whose talent is for living and loving in awe and worship.

Perhaps the whole of life is concerned with this yearning. Nothing can be left out, but it carries us on into death and beyond when we dare to hope that we shall come face to face with the source of all our longing.

From **Longing and Listening** *by* E. B., BBC Radio 'Epilogue'

'Thou hast made us for Thyself and our hearts are restless till they find rest in Thee.' Saint Augustine's words give us the clue to the longing which has been put into all our hearts and for which the whole of our life knowingly or unknowingly is a searching.

Georges Lefebvre in his book *Simplicity* puts this truth most clearly.

> God's fulness is present in the desire he awakens in our hearts. . . . This longing is most secret but also most strong. It is what is truest in us. . . . The Lord knows what is in our hearts. It is His work, the work of grace . . . in our silence he finds a prayer we may not know about. We offer him our silence.
> He gives us life and light.

From **Prayers of Grief and Glory** *by* Richard Harries

Some people are strongly aware of a longing for something more in experiences of beauty. Beauty both satisfies and leaves us restless for something beyond itself. As Simone Weil once put it, writing of something beautiful, 'We do not desire anything else, we possess it, and yet we still desire something. We do not in the least know what it is. We want to get behind beauty but it is only a surface. It is a sphinx, an enigma, a mystery which is painfully tantalising.'

But one great practical difficulty arises. How can we love what we don't see and can't imagine? For most there is only one way. We have to love the eternal as it makes itself known in and through the temporal. Take the flowers that come out with such colourful exuberance. Do we find them glorious? Their glory is only the humblest thread in the coat of divine glory. Kneeling alone in a room do we find stillness and peace? It is but a whisper from the endless forests of divine stillness. If there is beauty, peace, love to be found in this world how much more, oh how much more, is it to be found in God. And what we love in the world about us not only points beyond itself, but it bodies forth and conveys what is beyond to us. . . In the love of others divine love breaks through; in the beauty of the world, divine beauty can be glimpsed. As Simone Weil put it, 'The beauty of the world is Christ's tender smile for us coming through matter.' If we can find anything to love in the world we can begin to love the God who meets us in and through what we love.

By Jean Paul, *quoted in* **Springs of Consolation**

Without a divinity there is for man neither purpose, goal, nor hope, only a trembling future and eternal fear of the dark.

From **Each in His Own Tongue** *by* W. H. Carruth

POEM

Like tides on a crescent seabeach
When the moon is new and thin.
Into our heart's high yearnings
Come welling and surging in
Come from the mystic ocean
Whose rim no foot has trod
Some of us call it longing
And others call it God.

Matthew 13:44–6, Authorized Version

THE HID TREASURE

Again, the kingdom of heaven is like unto treasure hid in a field; the which when a man hath found, he hideth, and for joy thereof goeth and selleth all that he hath, and buyeth that field.

THE PEARL

Again, the kingdom of heaven is like unto a merchant man, seeking goodly pearls: Who, when he had found one pearl of great price, went and sold all that he had, and bought it.

From **Collected Poems** by A. E.

DESIRE

With thee a moment ! Then what dreams have play,
Traditions of eternal toil arise,
Search for the high, austere and lonely way
The Spirit moves in through eternities.
Ah, in the soul what memories arise!

And with what yearning inexpressible,
Rising from long forgetfulness I turn
To Thee, invisible, unrumoured, still:
White for Thy Whiteness all desires burn.
Ah, with what longing once again I turn!

From **Through Prayer to Reality** *by* Douglas A. Rhymes

Again do we find that our professed Christian desires are really at variance with our actual desires for life? There is a telling phrase in the Psalms, 'Thou gavest them their heart's desires and sent leanness withal into their souls' (Psalm 106:15). How terribly true this phrase is. Often we do, in fact, receive what we really desire, not what we feel we ought to desire, and the result is that our whole personalities become dwarfed and stunted. John Burnaby writes, 'God's children may not approach their Father with a feigned devotion fearing to tell Him what they truly want. I am to face with all the honesty I can achieve the real truth about my desires, to wrestle with the sham of professing desires which are not really mine. The schooling of desire is indeed prayer.' It is no good praying for humility if what I really want is power and success; it is no good praying for the guidance of the Holy Spirit if what I really want is to persuade someone to accept my own ideas; it is no good praying for love if what I really want is simply to go to bed with someone. Through prayer we can move from the world of fantasy to reality. Yet how do I know when I am in the world of reality rather than fantasy? Only in so far as my dreams accord with my actions and my will; otherwise they remain in the clouds—a land of feigned professions and wishful thinking.

From **Poems of Felicity** *by* Thomas Traherne

DESIRE

For giving me desire,
An eager thirst, a burning, ardent fire,
A virgin infant flame,
A love with which into the world I came,
An inward hidden heavenly love,
Which in my soul did work and move,
And ever, ever, me inflame
With restless longing, heavenly avarice,
That never could be satisfied,
That did incessantly a Paradise
Unknown suggest, and something undescried
Discern, and bear me to it; be
Thy name for ever praised by me . . .

This soaring, sacred thirst,
Ambassador of bliss, approached first,
Making a place in me
That made me apt to prize, and taste, and see;
For not the objects but the sense
Of things doth bliss to souls dispense,
And make it, Lord, like thee.
Sense, feeling, taste, complacency, and sight.
These are the true and real joys,
The living, flowing, inward, melting, bright,
And heavenly pleasures; all the rest are toys;
All which are founded in desire,
As light in flame, and heat in fire.

From **The Inward Road and the Way Back**
by Dorothee Soelle

A yearning is aroused within us to search for something that is not in this world. The loss which is the starting point of so many fairy tales and which happens under even the happiest and most fortunate of circumstances, cannot be set aright even in the fairy tales.

At the very outset there is a life-threatening situation that compels the hero to set out in search of what is missing. Nothing that originates in this world can satisfy or still this quest. Absolutely nothing that can be manufactured or purchased can compare with the 'golden bird' or the 'water of life' or the 'red flower'. That which is sought simply cannot be manufactured or produced nor can it be possessed or used up. Rather what is sought has to 'be experienced'.

. . . This quest is the yearning for the absolute, Man's wishes go beyond earthly fulfillment, beyond everything conceivable, and transcend all the limitations of time and space, gravity and causality. . . . Religion is to be found there where man's deepest desires and yearnings have been dreamed. By deepest desires and yearnings I mean those that cannot be fulfilled empirically. Horkheimer speaks of 'man's need for a state of eternal unending blessedness', a need which is apparent even among those moderns who reject the resurrection of the dead, the final judgement, and eternal life as dogmatic statements. This need itself cannot be relativized or made up for or destroyed.

. . . In order to make clearer what is involved I would like to remind the reader of the artist and the artistic method. Here, too, there is an absolute which cannot be fulfilled, a yearning for perfection, a suffering at having only a part, not the whole, the incomplete, that which is not well stated but which is always in the old language of the old man. All art involves the wish to go beyond what is to something more than this, more than all that is known.

'Nor eye hath seen, nor ear hath yet attained to hear, What there is ours. But we rejoice . . .' The mystics had forms of speech that express just this. The desire for another language, a language different from our ravaged and defiled double-speak, is an indication of this yearning. . . . The yearning for the absolute is enkindled at life's boundary points, mortality, death, guilt, suffering. But it does not flourish at these points. It is specifically the happy man who in the very midst of a full and rich life is driven on in the quest for fulfillment.

From **Selected Poems** *by* Mervyn Peake

OUT OF THE CHAOS OF MY DOUBT

Out of the chaos of my doubt
And the chaos of my art
I turn to you inevitably
As the needle to the pole
Turns . . . as the cold brain to the soul
Turns in its uncertainty;

So I turn and long for you;
So I long for you, and turn
To the love that through my chaos
Burns a truth
And lights my path.

By Bertrand Russell, *quoted in* **Springs of Consolation**

The man who centres
his thoughts
and hopes upon
something
transcending self
can find a certain
peace amidst the
ordinary troubles
of life which is
impossible to the
pure egoist.

From **The Rosemary Tree** *by* Elizabeth Goudge

Beauty awakens such intolerable longing that people often shut their eyes to it unaware that the longing was the greatest treasure that they had, their very life line, uniting the country of their lost innocence with the heavenly country for which their sails were set.

From **A Pattern of Faith** *by* Sister Edna Mary *and* Michael Marshall

The inability to recapture past reaction to beauty is common experience; even if one can see the same scene, hear the same music or poetry, the experience is different from what was remembered.

. . . On the human level there can be only the search for further experiences of beauty, and never final satisfaction.

. . . The more one grasps at something which has given pleasure, the more elusive it is; what one holds is not the thing itself but the container that once held it.

. . . If Wordsworth had gone back to those moments in the past, he would not have found the thing itself, but only the reminder of it. '. . . The books or the music in which we thought the beauty was located will betray us if we trust to them; it was not *in* them, it only came *through* them, and what came through them was longing. These things—the beauty, the memory of our own past—are good images of what we really desire; but if they are mistaken for the thing itself they turn into dumb idols, breaking the hearts of their worshippers. For they are not the thing itself; they are only the scent of a flower we have not found, the echo of a tune we have not yet heard, news from a country we have never yet visited' (C. S. Lewis).

From **Rediscovering Prayer** *by* John Casteel

WHERE PRAYING BEGINS

Men turn to prayer in the extremity of their fears, or anxieties, or helplessness before the perils of their day, and of all human existence. But they also turn to prayer because of the almost universal and unquenchable yearning they have for God, and for that fulness of life to be found in knowing, loving and serving Him.

This hunger for God will be described by every generation in its own language. In the seventeenth century, Henry Scougal, that bright and gentle young Scot, expressed it in saying, 'The glorious things spoken of heaven may make even the carnal heart in love with it.' For some modern minds, the statement of the psychologist, C. G. Jung, may be more intelligible: 'Everyone's ultimate aim and strongest desire lie in developing the fulness of human existence that is called personality'—a goal, as he points out, to be realized through the establishment of a personal relation between the human personality and a Power outside itself. Dorothy Day, a distinguished Catholic laywoman, speaks experientially of this hunger, as she knew it even in her childhood, by quoting the words of Kiriloff, in Dostoevsky's novel, *The Possessed*: 'All my life I have been haunted by God.' In every generation this interior restlessness, this mingling of impassioned longing with the intimation of bright hope, rekindles the inward being in men and women, until they move out to seek Him by whom that being, and that hunger, first were given us.

Nor is this longing after God confined to high moments of ecstasy and vision. A young man sitting down to plan and dream for his future—his career, his marriage, his achievement of professional success and social status—may appear to be thinking in quite material terms. Income, prospects, and connections may seem to be the centre of his anticipation and his calculation as to how they are to be achieved and employed. Yet even as he speaks of these practical considerations, the light in his eyes and the nuance of his voice betrays a larger, unguessed hope, whose aura flames about his dreams.

From **Songs of the Lover and the Beloved**
by E. Allison Peers

A HYMN

O Heavenly Beauty, lovelier far
Than any beauty we can know.
On starriest night thou fairest star
Thou light most glorious from below,
Thou hidden world with radiant glow!

O heavenly Truth, that here dost shine
A beacon-light our path to guide,
Set by a hand unseen, Divine
To all revealed, to none denied,
On high yet ever at our side!

Beacon ahead and star above:
To such a journey both are one-
One, too, with mystic fire of love
Consuming flame that stays for none-
For all are kindled by the sun.

Lord God of Light no strength have we
To walk securely on our way,
But our desires are known to thee:
By beacon then and star we pray
Lead us through night to glorious day.

From **Psalm 107,** Book of Common Prayer

Then are they glad, because they are at rest:
and so he bringeth them to a haven where they would be.

Longing *by* Naomi Blake

Man's needs, desires, and his longing for personal happiness—yet on the other side Man's tendencies for self-destruction. Mass graves, tortures, ruthless wars, weapons getting more and more lethal. What is stronger in us, the longing for progress in medicine and technology, to develop, to better man, or to destroy him by wars in the name of defence and survival? What is the purpose of life, to preserve, or to destroy? Are we longing for one or the other? Or is there a harmonious balance that we are really looking for? Is the longing ever fulfilled?

Did Magda experience it in 1944 in Auschwitz concentration camp?

She lay in the barrack on her bunk, weak, helpless; fingers, lips, tongue swollen to twice their normal size. At '*appel*' (roll call), hungry and cold as she was, she couldn't swallow even the watery porridge she got for breakfast. The thin slice of bread that went with the porridge, she usually kept for later. Like most of the inmates, she kept it in her hand, so that nobody could steal it. She lay there on the bunk, her whole body aching, waiting anxiously for something, terror stricken, demented, waiting. The waves of terror recurred every time on a greater scale than before. In her mind, to survive—to tell the tale—was a kind of life-line. Scared out of her wits—trembling—ears straining to catch the murmur of passing noises—fear-contorted—faces all around her, struck from the ranks of human beings—stripped of their names and numbered.

Suddenly—commotion, awful inhuman cries from outside; '*heraus*' ('out, out'). Like a shot they were out, hundreds of them, pushing towards the exit not to be among the last. For those who faltered or stumbled were savagely beaten by the guards or torn by the dogs. Magda, holding her piece of bread in her hand, was pushed and hurried out of the barrack, chased with the others through the camp. Panic-stricken she ran, her whole body aching. Out of sheer terror she ran with great speed in the deep snow—the biting wind, the hard blows from the whips, the barking of the dogs, the inhuman cries around her. A swift glance back revealed bodies on the ground, patches of blood on the snow, people shot by the guards or torn by the dogs, for not being able to keep up with the rest.

And then it happened. How long she ran, when she stopped, and for how long she couldn't tell. Nor could she remember how she got back to her bunk. The only thing that stuck in her mind was her tremendous longing for all this to stop, for peace, quiet, warmth, for her to enjoy the piece of bread. To be alone. There leaning against a fence, she felt a curious fulfilment. All her sensations came to a stop, aches, fears, terrors, vanished beyond somewhere. She felt a sweet comfort eating her bread, amidst the noise, the cries, the running. She heard nothing, saw nothing, yet aware of everything, body and soul harmonious, at complete peace with herself. It was as if all her longing came to fulfilment.

Magda survived to tell the tale. Many years have gone by since then. The camp has been ever present in her mind. She tried to push into oblivion events of those hideous days. This one event she cannot forget, nor does she want to, for it shines like a torch in the night, before her inner eyes, as a proof that good and not evil will prevail in the end.

From **Revelations of Divine Love** *by* Julian of Norwich

LOVE, LONGING AND PITY

I saw that God can do all that we need. These three we need: love, longing and pity. Pity and love keep us in the time of our need. And the longing in the same love draweth us unto heaven. For God thirsteth to have all-man, generally, in himself. In which thirst he hath drawn up all his holy souls that are now in bliss. And in gaining his living members, ever he draweth up and drinketh; and yet he still thirsteth and longeth.

From **Collected Poems** *by* W. H. Auden

FOR THE TIME BEING

And because of His visitation we may no longer desire God as if He were lacking: our redemption is no longer a question of pursuit but of surrender to Him who is always and everywhere present. Therefore at every moment we pray that, following Him, we may depart from our anxiety into His peace.

Part II

LIVING

LOVING

LAUGHTER and JOY

LIVING

'God make me to be involved in life but keep me part of you'

From **Venture to the Interior** *by* Laurens van der Post

LETTER FROM INGARET GIFFARD

It seems to me that people's private and personal lives have never mattered as they do now. For me the whole of the future depends on the way people live their personal rather than their collective lives. It is a matter of extreme urgency. When we have all lived out our private and personal problems we can consider the next, the collective step. Then it will be easy but before it will not even be possible.

From **Markings** *by* Dag Hammarskjöld

Each day the first day: each day a life.
Each morning we must hold out the chalice of our being to receive, to carry, and give back. It must be held out empty—for the past must only be reflected in its polish, its shape, its capacity . . . and those things which for our unworthiness we dare not, and for our blindness we cannot ask, vouchsafe to give us.
(The Book of Common Prayer, General Collect).

A Very Old Chinese Proverb.

If there be righteousness
in the heart, there will be
beauty in the character.
If there is beauty in the
character there will be
harmony in the home.
If there is harmony in the
home, there will be order
in the nation.
When there is order in each nation
there will be peace in the world.

From Conversations With Kafka *by* Gustav Janouch

'All true art is a document, a statement of evidence,' said Franz Kafka gravely. 'A people with children like those in the book (Tashkent, the Bountiful City) a people like that can never go under.'

'Perhaps it does not depend on individuals.'

'On the contrary! The species of matter is determined by the number of electrons in the atom. The level of the masses depends on the consciousness of individuals.'

From A Gift Of Light *by* Father Andrew

NATURE OF CHRISTIAN LIFE

Because our God is, as St Paul said, 'The God of Hope' we shall join hope to faith, and both to love. We could not have a hopeless faith any more than we could have a faithless love. If hope will go to school at Calvary, hope may learn to become a fellow-scholar with Dismas the thief, and to see the kingdom coming even though the King be crowned with thorns.

While we learn some of the secrets of faith and hope, we shall learn also to know that when the light of faith dims down and that of hope seems to be extinguished, the light of true love need never lose the least portion of its radiance, but may shine on in darkness, and gain perhaps a truer radiance from that darkness. Faith will teach us prayer, hope will teach us service, love will teach us consecration and worship and bring to faith its beauty and to hope its wings.

Romans 15:13 *from* **The New Testament in Modern English** *by* J. B. Phillips

May the God of hope fill *you* with joy and peace in your faith, that by the power of the Holy Spirit, your whole life and outlook may be radiant with hope.

From the **Confessions** *of* St Augustine

But thou wilt give light to my lantern, O Lord my God, thou wilt lighten my darkness, and of thy fulness have we all received. For thou art the true Light which illuminateth every man coming into this world, because in thee there is no transmutation nor shadow of change.

From **The Fate of Empires and the Search for Survival** *by* John Glubb

THE SPIRIT MAKES ALIVE

The effect of spirit

In all problems, it is not the cleverness of the planning which can ensure success, but the spirit which inspires the persons involved. Love will always find a way. Love we are told, is patient and benevolent, is not jealous or arrogant, or selfish, and is not easily provoked. To some extent, the present ideals of the British Commonwealth are based on this spirit, if its leaders can live up to it. Above all it means not to use compulsion, except in the very last resort—that is, if it is the only way to protect the weak from the most terrible forms of oppression.

A revival of religion

I am convinced that moral standards can only be raised by a revival of religion. The proliferation of '-isms' in our own times proves that no intellectual panacea can command general support. A group of clever people produce a theory of society which they are convinced will result in an earthly paradise, but it is impossible to build a dream society with violent, selfish people. Their theories are bitterly attacked by other groups, and conflict and hatred result.

Religion alone can persuade men to abandon their immediate, short-term selfishness and to dedicate themselves to the common good in complete self-oblivion. By religion, I mean the conviction that this life is not the end; that there is a spiritual world which, though invisible, penetrates all creation, and which can strike a sympathetic note in every human heart.

To accept the existence of this vast spiritual world immensely enlarges our horizon and enables us to see the pettiness of our quarrels and our attempts to grab for ourselves. It can result in a gradual transformation of our characters. But more often than not, pride in our own cleverness closes our minds to the spiritual world which everywhere surrounds and envelops us.

Prayer for Service *by* E. B.

O Lord, put the spirit of service into our hearts.
Give us, we beseech thee, the desire to serve thee,
The desire to serve others, the desire to be of service to the world.
And then do thou give us the wisdom to see where and when we can be of service and the humility and grace to accept gratefully the service of others.

From **A Vision of the Aquarian Age** *by* George Trevelyan

A quotation from Sri Aurobindo, published in the Auroville Magazine, One:

We must remember that this is a call to the young in heart, however many years they may have lived, for the soul within us is immortal and ageless.

OUR CALL IS TO THE YOUNG

The future belongs to the young.
It is a young and new world which is now under process of development
And it is the young who must create it.
But it is also a world of truth, courage, justice, lofty aspirations and straightforward fulfillment
which we seek to create.
Our ideal is a new birth of humanity into the spirit;
our life must be a spiritually inspired effort
to create a body of action for the great new birth and creation.
Our ideal is not the spirituality that withdraws from life
but the conquest of life by the power of the spirit
It is to accept the world as an effort of manifestation
of the Divine,
but also to transform humanity
by a greater effort of manifestation than has yet been accomplished,
one in which the veil between man and God shall be removed, the divine manhood of which we are capable shall come to birth and our life shall be remolded in the truth and light and power of the spirit.
It is the young who are free in mind and heart
to accept a completer truth and labour for a greater ideal.
They must be men who will dedicate themselves not to the past or the present
but to the future.
They will need to consecrate their lives to an exceeding of their lower self,
to the realisation of God in themselves and in all human beings
and to a whole-hearted and indefatigable labour for the nation and for humanity.
This ideal can be as yet only a little seed and the life that embodies it a small nucleus,
but it is our fixed hope that the seed will grow into a tree and the nucleus be the heart of an ever-extending formation.
It is with a confident trust in the spirit that inspires us that we take our place
among the standard-bearers of the new humanity that is struggling to be born.

From **God's a Good Man and Other Poems**
by Monica Furlong

A slum is where somebody else lives,
Help is what others need.
We all want to be the priest, social worker, nurse,
The nun in the white habit giving out the soup—
To work from a position of power,
The power being
That we are not the shuffler in the queue
Holding out his bowl.

But there is only one way into the kingdom
To be found out in our poverty.
That is why the citizens are a job lot—
Unhappily married, the feckless mother of eight,
The harlot no longer young,
The lover of little girls, the sexually untameable,
The alcoholic, the violent and those whose drink is despair.
Show me not, Lord, your rich men
With their proud boasts of poverty and celibacy
They are too much for me.
Hide me from those who want to help
And still have strength to do so.
Only those who get on with their lives
And think they have nothing to give
Are any use to me.
Let your bankrupts feed me.

From **An Anthology of the Love of God**
by Evelyn Underhill

SYMPATHY THE HEIGHT OF LOVE

. . . Christ never criticised any but the respectable and pious: with every one else His thought went like a shaft of delight straight to something He could admire—the love of the prostitute, the meekness of the publican, the faith of the centurion, the confidence of the penitent thief—all things which irradiate and save humanity. Love looks for those first, and one reason why Christ gives us rest, is that in His presence we are bound to love—not to criticise.

From **Fruit Gathering** *by* Rabindranath Tagore

Let me not pray to be sheltered from dangers but to be fearless in facing them.
Let me not beg for the stilling of my pain but for the heart to conquer it. . . .
Let me not crave in anxious fear to be saved but hope for the patience to win my freedom.
Grant me that I may not be a coward, feeling your mercy in my success alone; but let me find the grasp of your hand in my failure.

From **The Zodiac Arch** *by* Freya Stark

. . . Whatever the abyss from which it comes, the darkness of pain is here in our sunniest landscape, a blot no government can tackle or science dispel. Our frame of security must find room for sorrow, together with cruelty and death; and no welfare state can do more than make us tolerably comfortable while things go tolerably well.

Yet in beauty unimaginable, beauty in every opening leaf untouched by fear, we would never look beyond the radiance of our world if sorrow were not its inhabitant. The angels might be about us, and we would not see them: we would be in prison and not know it; and whatever Divinity there is would walk in His garden alone. Nothing but the transitory will make man look for the eternal, nor will he ever accept the one as substitute for the other, for such is the innate nobility of man. His human dignity, his attribute of pain, his crown of thorns is no bridge across chaos: but nothing else can make him look to see if a bridge is there. This precious incentive he will not consent to lose, whatever the cost may be. And let Martha by all means look to our earthly comfort, for we need it badly; but let her not call it security.

From **A Vision of the Aquarian Age** *by* George Trevelyan

Whenever one permits oneself to express discouragement, criticism, cynicism, anger or fear, one sends out a jet of darkness into the already darkened psychic atmosphere of the world—which in consequence, rebounds back on us to our own further detriment.

Conversely, whenever one takes the initiative and attempts to build high-self positive qualities into the soul, one strengthens the bond with the planes of light. This is our human duty and purpose. It has been contended that we are the vocabulary we use. We are obviously free to choose to cut out all negative expressions. If we allow none such to pass our lips, we will in time eradicate them from our thoughts as well. We can, in short, learn to use what has been called the 'perfect language'.

Meditation is a channel for continuous reconstitution of the self, to prepare it that it may move into the new. . . . The entire nervous system and the vital processes rest as in deep sleep, while there is a condition of alert attention in the mind, a listening to the world of being. We are then open to the qualities of the Higher Self, which essentially are peace, love, gentleness, courage and joy.

While these fill the soul, there is simply no room for the negative qualities of the lower self, which include remorse, regret, disappointment, anger, resentment for things past, and fear, anxiety and doubt about the future. These negative emotions cannot enter, any more than darkness can remain in a room when we switch on the light.

From **Peak in Darien** *by* Freya Stark

This passion for the surface of the world was satisfied for many years by mountain climbing. It taught me one of the basic rules of travel—to carry all one needs and nothing more—and gave that taste for space in its own right which can destroy a nomad in captivity and could, I believe, kill many other people too, if there were no means to create the open world inside one.

From **A One Hour Service for Good Friday** *by* C. I. Pettitt

We bring our work to your working hands;
We bring our sickness to your healing hands;
We bring our weakness to your strong hands;
We bring our sadness to your tender hands;
We bring our needs to your praying hands;
We bring our suffering to your wounded hands;

We bring our love, our families and our children to your hands
outstretched to bless;
We bring our hands to share with you
that bread of life which we take
from you, that we may take your
sacramental presence to share with others.
As we take your hands, we are to be those hands in the world
today.

From **Love's Endeavour, Love's Expense** *by* W. H. Vanstone

In the concrete reality of existence man is aware of triumph as well as tragedy. There is a time to laugh as well as a time to weep. Though many are hungry many are also fed. Though many are homeless many are happy in their homes. The reality of triumph in one situation is not denied by the reality of tragedy in another: nor can the joy and strength of triumph always be expended in the redemption of tragedy. Sometimes triumph can be so expended—as when the joy of a happy home is put at risk in order that a homeless family may share it, or when a man jeopardises his own strength in the care of an invalid. But the possibilities of freedom are limited: and often there is no way in which triumph can serve to redeem or alleviate tragedy. It is a mere affectation of sensitivity when a man claims that, so long as there is tragedy anywhere in the world he himself can feel no joy; or that so long as there is redemptive work, however distant, to be done, he himself will know no rest. In many a concrete situation there is something to spare of triumph and of joy which cannot possibly be expended for the redeeming of tragedy: there is a measure of freedom, of 'leisure', which is unchallenged by the needs and distresses of the surrounding world. Realistically seen, the life of the most 'dedicated' man contains a measure of such freedom: the life of most men contains huge areas of it.

Prayer *by* Blaise Pascal

Teach us, O Lord to do the little things as though they were great because of the majesty of Christ who does them in us and who lives our life; and to do the greatest things as though they were little and easy because of his omnipotence.

From The Book of Zohar

God conceals himself from the mind of man, but reveals himself to his heart.

Jewish Proverb

He who wants to live his life should equip himself with a heart which can stand suffering. Man must realize that life is sometimes good and sometimes bad. Only he is worthy of respect who is grateful for the good and knows how to bear evil.

By Franz Kafka, *quoted in* Springs of Jewish Wisdom

Man cannot live without a lasting trust in something indestructible within him, but both his trust and its indestructible object can remain forever concealed from him. One expression of this concealment is man's faith in a personal God.

From Experiment in Depth *by* P. W. Martin

The man who lives from the deep centre discovers a new dynamic. He is worked *through* in a manner wholly different from his previous experience.

The energy coming from the deep centre is not subject to the law of opposites. It is quiet. This is not to say that the man through whom the energy flows lives a life of placid ease. He has to strive and agonise at the conscious level, more so than before perhaps. But he does not agonise for nothing.

New and creative springs of action arise in the depths; and in the midst of his striving the man finds himself serving *as a channel by which they find their way into life.*

From **A Gift Of Light** *by* Father Andrew

SILENCES

How many silences there are—
  The winter's white tranquillity;
The silver silence of a star;
  The moon's pure queenly sovereignty;

The awful silences of hate;
  Still water's deep profundity;
The silent swiftness of the spate;
  And all sly, crouching cruelty;

The silence of the dawning day;
  The velvet silence of the night;
Their silence who have learned to pray;
  The silence of the Infinite.

The sweet green silence of the glade;
  Blue silences of twilight dear;
Their silence who are not afraid
  And wait for Truth their cause to clear;

The silence of the Stable Cave,
  When all His visitors had gone
And He slept sound Who came to save,
  And Mary pondered there alone;

The silence when He bowed His head
  After the loud last bitter cry,
When Mary knew her Babe was dead
  And the sun set on Calvary;

The silence of the Garden shrine
  Beneath the star-strewn Syrian sky,
Where lay the Lord of life divine,
  Wrapped in death's silent mystery.

How many silences there are,
  In earth below, in heaven above,
And best and sweetest of them far,
  The golden silences of love.

From **The Inward Road and the Way Back** *by* Dorothee Soelle

To believe in God means to take sides with life and to end our alliance with death. It means to stop killing and wanting to kill, and to do battle with apathy which is so akin to killing. It means an end to the fear of dying and to its counterpart, the fear of failure. To take sides with life means to stop looking for some neutral ground between murderers and their victims and to cease looking upon the world as a supermarket in which we can buy anything we want so long as the price is right and the system is preserved.

Taking sides with life is not an easy or simple thing. It involves a never-ending process of change whereby we constantly renounce the self that is dead and enamoured of death and instead become free to love life. To take sides with life and experience how we can transcend ourselves is a process that has many names and faces. Religion is one of those names. Religion can mean the radical and wholehearted attempt to take sides with life.

From **Markings** *by* Dag Hammarskjöld

So, once again, you chose for yourself—and opened the door to chaos. The chaos you become whenever God's hand does not rest upon your head.

From **The English Poems of George Herbert**

AFFLICTION

Broken in pieces all asunder,
  Lord, hunt me not,
  A thing forgot,
Once a poore creature, now a wonder,
  A wonder tortur'd in the space
  Betwixt this world and that of grace.

My thoughts are all a case of knives,
  Wounding my heart
  With scatter'd smart,

As watering pots give flowers their lives,
  Nothing their furie can controll,
  While they do wound and prick my soul.

All my attendants are at strife,
  Quitting their place
  Unto my face:
Nothing performs the task of life:
  The elements are let loose to fight,
  And while I live, trie out their right.

Oh help, my God! let not their plot
  Kill them and me,
  And also thee,
Who art my life: dissolve the knot,
  As the sunne scatters by his light
  All the rebellions of the night.

Then shall those powers, which work for grief,
  Enter thy pay,
  And day by day
Labour thy praise, and my relief;
  With care and courage building me
  Till I reach heav'n and much more thee.

From **The Reed Of God** *by* Caryll Houselander

Today Christ is dependent upon men. In the Host He is literally put into a man's hands. A man must carry Him to the dying, must take Him into the prisons, work houses and hospitals, must carry Him in a tiny pyx over the heart on to the field of battle, must give Him to little children and 'lay Him by' in His 'leaflight' house of gold.

. . . This dependence of Christ lays a great trust upon us. . . . We must carry Him in our hearts to wherever He wants to go, and there are many places to which He may never go unless we take Him to them.

. . . Sometimes it may seem to us that there is no purpose in our lives, that going day after day for years to this office or that school or factory is nothing else but waste and weariness. But it may be that God has sent us there because but for us Christ would not be there. If our being there means that Christ is there, that alone makes it worth while.

Prayer *by* Gary Davies

Thank you, Lord for strength to match our weakness, comfort to lighten our distress, guidance to lead us in perplexity, inner peace to hold us against disaster, love to dissolve our bitterness and forgiveness to cover our failure. So much has been given to us. Help us to bring hope to the despair of others.

From **The Dynamics of Repentence** *by* Edward Aubert

REPENTANCE, REMORSE AND HEALING

If repentence is to be fully effective, the importance of the part played by forgiveness must be understood. Many people fail to benefit from forgiveness in the way they should, because the therapeutic energies which are thereby released become blocked by a failure to understand what forgiveness really means. It means, first of all, that the *relationship* between One's self and God has been restored. That this relationship is of supreme importance is acknowledged by the late Professor Jung, who writes in his book 'Psychology and Religion': 'During the past thirty years people from all the civilised countries of the world have consulted me. Among all my patients in the second half of life—that is to say over thirty-five—there has not been one whose problem in the last resort was not that of finding a religious outlook on life. It is safe to say that every one of them fell ill because he had lost that which the living religions of every age have given to their followers, and none of them has been really healed who did not regain his religious outlook. Side by side with the decline of religious life, the neuroses grow noticeably more frequent.'

We may not be the same as we were before we sinned, we may even be suffering from various consequences of our sin, but the relationship is restored. We can begin afresh, as though we had never sinned. The Bible speaks of our sins as being 'blotted out', as 'remembered no more for ever'.

. . . The act of repentence is something which we choose to undertake. It is therefore an act of the will. The will is not given its fair share of attention by modern psychology. Instead the behaviourists are doing their best to deprive man of any will at all, by reducing his activities to the level of instinct and reflex response.

It is precisely this faculty—the will—which is shackled by a sense of sin. Before repentence the will is divided, and such activity as takes place cannot be whole-hearted. But after repentence the will can be unified and one-pointed, turned in a new direction.

Prayer

You have given me life, Lord, and a world full of people to care for and you have promised that nothing can tear me from your love. What more can I want, Lord? You have given me all!

From **Between Man and Man** *by* Martin Buber

Consider a typical peasant, as he still exists, although the social and cultural conditions for his existence seem to have disappeared; it happens that on his day off he can be seen standing there staring into the clouds, and if asked he replies, after a while, that he has been studying the weather, and you see that it is not true. At the same time he can occasionally be seen with his mouth quite unexpectedly opening—to utter a saying. Before this he had of course uttered sayings, but traditional and known ones, which were mostly humorously pessimistic utterances about 'the way of things'. He still utters the same kind now, but he makes, time and again, remarks of a quite different kind, such as were not heard from him earlier and unknown to tradition. And he utters them staring ahead, often only whispering as though to himself; they can barely be caught; he is uttering his own insights. He does not do this when he has experienced the contrariness of things, but for example when the ploughshare has sunk softly and deeply into the soil as though the furrow were deliberately opening to receive it, or when the cow has been quickly and safely delivered of her calf as though an invisible power were helping. That is, he utters his own insights if he has experienced the grace of things, if he has once again experienced despite all contrariness that man participates in the being of the world.

The Farmer's Prayer

When we are careless with the beasts and forget they are
God's creatures:
When we are unkind to men, and forget they are
God's children
When we ill-treat the land, and forget it is the
splendour of God:
O God forgive us.

From The Life Radiant *by* Lilian Whiting

Anxiety and misgiving, wrote Fénélon, proceed solely from love of self. The love of God accomplishes all things quietly and completely, it is not anxious or uncertain. The spirit of God rests continually in quietness. Perfect love casteth out fear. It is in forgetfulness of self that we find peace. Happy is he who yields himself completely, unconsciously, and finally to God. Listen to the inward whisper of His Spirit and follow it—that is enough; but to listen one must be silent and to follow one must yield.

From Markings *by* Dag Hammarskjöld

With the love of Him who knows all,
With the patience of Him whose now is eternal,
With the righteousness of Him who has never failed,
With the humility of Him who has suffered all the
possibilities of betrayal.

From The Spirit in Man, Art, and Literature *by* C. G. Jung

At this point the *I Ching* responds to something in us that is in need of further development. Occultism has enjoyed a renaissance in our times that is without parallel—the light of the Western mind is nearly darkened by it. I am not thinking now of our seats of learning and their representatives. As a doctor who deals with ordinary people, I know that the universities have ceased to act as disseminators of light. People are weary of scientific specialization and rationalism and intellectualism. They want to hear truths that broaden rather than restrict, that do not obscure but enlighten, that do not run off them like water but penetrate them to the marrow. This search is only too likely to lead a large if anonymous public astray.

. . . A beggar is not helped by having alms, great or small, pressed into his hand, even though this may be what he wants. He is far better helped if we show him how he can permanently rid himself of his beggary by work. Unfortunately the spiritual beggars of our time are too inclined to accept the alms of the East in bulk and to imitate its ways unthinkingly. This is a danger about which too many warnings cannot be uttered. . . . The spirit of Europe is not helped merely by new sensations or a titillation of the nerves. What it has taken China thousands of years to build cannot be acquired by theft. If we want to possess it, we must earn the right to it by working on ourselves. Of what use to us is the wisdom of the Upanishads or the insight of Chinese yoga if we desert our own foundations as though they were errors outlived, and, like homeless pirates, settle with thievish intent on foreign shores?

The insights of the East, and in particular the wisdom of The *I Ching*, have no meaning for us if we close our minds to our own problems, jog along with our conventional prejudices, and veil from ourselves our real human nature with all its dangerous undercurrents and darknesses. The light of this wisdom shines only in the dark, not in the brightly lit theatre of our European consciousness and will.

Attributed to Abraham Lincoln

You cannot bring about prosperity by discouraging thrift: you cannot strengthen the weak by weakening the strong; you cannot help the wage-earner by pulling down the wage-payer; you cannot further the brotherhood of man by encouraging class hatred; you cannot help the poor by destroying the rich; you cannot establish sound security on borrowed money; you cannot keep out of trouble by spending more than you earn; you cannot build character and courage by taking away man's initiative and independence; you cannot help men permanently by doing for them what they could and should do for themselves.

From **Perseus in the Wind** *by* Freya Stark

SERVICE

Service became the instrument not only of Christianity but of every religion in the world, long before houses or housemaids were invented. It was the rose in the first desert, and still makes life possible for nurses, government officials, men in offices, whose work might otherwise be arid beyond their capacity to bear. It endows humble people with their chance of the greatest of worldly luxuries, since it makes of their labour, which is the only commodity they have, a thing that can be given. And it is free from the dangers of philanthropy, since it is free from arrogance. Its secret of happiness is made manifest in any crisis, when men forget to care about their rights and think of service only.

By Katie Riley, *from an article in* **Quaker Monthly**

KATIE'S PRAYER

Desperately we commit to thy care the years of our life that are before us. Give us strength to be of service to our fellows. May our lives shine so that others feel the warmth of thy spirit.

It is the warmth of our spirit overflowing among others who seek, who are ill, who are lonely, for which we pray. We would become people who add to this small world's knowledge of Truth. People whose very presence heals. Tranquil people,in whom the loneliness of others is stilled.

We see through a glass darkly—but may we be given a vision that enables us to transmit through our own personality what we see of permanence and value. We realise that the meditations of our hearts influence not only ourselves, but others. We pray that our thoughts shall be pure, that their very purity may bring healing to ourselves and to others.

Often we lie in bed at night and toss and turn. May we be enabled to reach out to Christ, the centre of centres—and to find rest and stillness and having found it may we be enabled to radiate this stillness to others.

We pray from the depths of our hearts that we may be more worthy followers of thee. We pray to be absolved—to be made one—with all the goodness of the world. We know we are surrounded by an ocean of darkness but we know that there is an ocean of light. It is into this ocean of light that we desire to move, and into which we would carry our sick friends.

Help us, O God, to identify ourselves with all who suffer. yet help us to move forward with a gladness that is infectious. We pray that we may discover how to remain young, gay, enthusiastic, full of enterprise. A smile inward and outward; a means of facing with sweetness and gentleness whatever befalls us.

LOVING

'Love is life coupling together the lover and the loved'

From the introduction by Lumsden Barkway *to* **An Anthology of the Love of God** *by* Evelyn Underhill

Love is the cosmic energy that flames from the constellations and is concealed in the abyss of the atom; is whispered by the Holy Spirit in the heart, and placarded before men's eyes upon the Cross. It offers us all that it has, and demands from us all that we can give.

By Rainer Maria Rilke

Once the realisation is accepted that even between the closest human beings infinite distances continue to exist, a wonderful living side by side can grow up, if they succeed in loving the distance between them which makes it possible for each to see the other whole against the sky.

From **The Cosmic Christ** *by* Ladislaus Boros

. . . Our destiny and that of the world we inhabit was decided when Christ rose from the dead. . . . Nothing, Paul said in his letter to the Romans, will ever be able to separate us from the love of Christ (Rom. 8:35 ff.). Nothing—except a rejection of Christ's love. We have already attained freedom, openness, and joy. The Christ of the Apocalypse declared: 'I have set before you an open door, which no one is able to shut' (Rev. 3:8). Wherever a small flame of genuine love burns, there is the light of heaven, already visibly present. No hope is ever in vain. We lose nothing. Ultimately, we cannot lose anything that we go without in our lives on earth. We have no reason to be despondent or despairing. The whole of Christianity can, seen in this perspective, be summarized as the faith in which God says Yes to our longings, and goes so far beyond them that even our most audacious hopes and dreams sometimes seem faint-hearted and lacking in faith.

From **The Mystical Doctrine of St John of the Cross**

THE SPIRITUAL BETROTHAL

My Beloved is the mountains,
The solitary wooded valleys,
The strange islands,
The roaring torrents,
The whisper of the amorous gales;

The tranquil night
At the approaches of the dawn,
The silent music,
The murmuring solitude,
The supper which revives, and enkindles love.

From **Liber Amoris** *by* William Hazlitt

Perfect love has this advantage in it, that it leaves the possessor of it nothing farther to desire. There is one object (at least) in which the soul finds absolute content, for which it seeks to live or dares to die. The heart has, as it were, filled up the moulds of the imagination. The truth of passion keeps pace with and outvies the extravagance of mere language. There are no words so fine, no flattery so soft, that there is not a sentiment beyond them, that it is impossible to express, at the bottom of the heart where true love is.

From **Love's Endeavour, Love's Expense**
by W. H. Vanstone

The love of God must be infinitely more costly, more precarious and more exposed than it is commonly represented to be. . . If God is love, and if the universe is His creation then for the being of the universe God is totally expended in precarious endeavour, of which the issue, as triumph or tragedy, has passed from His hands. For that issue, as triumphant or as tragic, God waits upon the response of His creation. He waits as the artist or as the lover waits, having given all. Where the issue is tragedy, there remains only the unbelievable power of art or love to discover within itself, through the challenge of the tragic, the power which was not there before—the power of yet further endeavour to win back and redeem that which was going astray. Where the issue is triumph, there remains only the will of love to surrender triumphant self-sufficiency in yet larger, more distant, more generous endeavour. Always, for the richness of the creation, God is made poor: and for its fullness, God is made empty. Always His helplessness waits upon the response of creation. To anyone who does not understand this, or cannot accept it, we must answer, 'You have not yet weighed the cost of love, the cost of creation.'

• • •

If the creation is the work of love, its 'security' lies not in its conformity to some predetermined plan but in the unsparing love which will not abandon a single fragment of it, and man's assurance must be the assurance not that all that happens is determined by God's plan but that all that happens is encompassed by His love.

From **Sadhana,** *translated by* Rabindranath Tagore

This is my prayer to thee, my lord—strike, strike at the
  root of penury in my heart.
Give me the strength lightly to bear my joys and sorrows.
Give me the strength to make my love fruitful in service.
Give me the strength never to disown the poor or bend my knees
  before insolent might.
Give me the strength to raise my mind high above daily trifles.
And give me the strength to surrender my strength to thy will
  with love.

From **Longing and Listening** *by* E. B., BBC Radio 'Epilogue'

So often the longing shows itself in love for another person. Ben Jonson in his poem expresses the yearning through the natural things, through the senses, seeing, feeling, smelling, touching, and supremely in loving.

> Have you seen but a white lily grow before
> rude hands had touched it?
> Have you seen but the fall of the snow before the earth
> hath smutched it?
> Have you felt the wool of beaver or
> swan's down ever?
> Have you smelt the bud of the briar or
> the nard in the fire?
> Have you tasted the bag of the Bee?
> O so white! O so soft! O so sweet is she!

In his poem 'Station of the Globe', Thomas Blackburn reminds us that all human love is fulfilled and transcended by the love of God.

> No single station of the globe
> Can rest the urgency of love,
> Whose true vocation must exceed
> All pastures where its children feed,
> Transcending in one breathless act
> The possibilities of fact,
> We learn no mortal creature is
> The end of love's immensities.

From **Asolando** *by* Robert Browning

SUMMUM BONUM

All the breath and the bloom of the year in the bag of one bee:
All the wonder and wealth of the mine in the heart of one gem:
In the core of one pearl all the shade and the shine of the sea:
Breath and bloom, shade and shine, wonder, wealth, and—how far above them—
  Truth, that's brighter than gem,
  Trust, that's purer than pearl—
Brightest truth, purest trust in the universe—
  All were for me in the kiss of one girl.

By Robert Burns

THE WINTER

The Winter it is past, and the summer is come at last
And the small birds, they sing on every tree;
Now ev'ry thing is glad, while I am very sad
Since my true love is parted from me.

The rose upon the brier, by the waters running clear,
May have charms for the linnet or the bee;
Their little loves are blest, and their little hearts at rest,
But my true love is parted from me.

From **The Moment of Truth** *by* Ladislaus Boros

MYSTERIUM MORTIS

What actually happens to a person in those very rare moments in which the force of his love goes out—even though it be but fleetingly—towards another human being in such a way that this other is affirmed by him, and affirmed with all the fulness of his life? A situation is then dimly perceived as existing, and it is even attained for just a moment in a flaring up of the spirit, that can be described as follows: in the ecstasy of love no self-enrichment is sought or indeed experienced, even in a secondary way. If it were necessary and possible, the lover could sacrifice all self-enrichment to his love. This can go so far that his own love is not experienced in any way as 'his', but is received in a spirit of unutterable humility as pure gift. As the old French saying has it; '*C'est moi qui te dois tout, puisque c'est moi qui t'aime.*'

In these moments—even though it is not a lasting emotion—there occurs a surrender that is complete. The person has given himself, and held himself back only in so far as this was necessary for the gift offered. Whatever such a man still hopes for in life, he expects to receive for the sake of the other person. He hopes for something for himself so that he can give it to the other: '*J'espère en toi pour nous.*' By this attitude the terrible self-centredness of existence is resolved, and man stands free as pure gift. Of course such moments are fleeting and unstable. Existence falls back at once into itself and begins to fail in its self-giving. The wall of self is once more built up and must in loyalty be broken through again and again. Man is capable of delivering himself up to another in this way only in the most sublime, most generous hours of his life, and of 'being' in this act of self-surrender for only a fleeting moment.

By William Shakespeare

SONNET CXVI

Let me not to the marriage of true minds
Admit impediments. Love is not love
Which alters when it alteration finds,
Or bends with the remover to remove.
O, no! it is an ever-fixed mark,
That looks on tempests and is never shaken;
It is the star to every wand'ring bark,
Whose worth's unknown, although his height be taken.
Love's not Time's fool, though rosy lips and cheeks
Within his bending sickle's compass come;
Love alters not with his brief hours and weeks,
But bears it out even to the edge of doom.
  If this be error, and upon me prov'd,
  I never writ, nor no man ever lov'd.

From **Travelling In** *by* Monica Furlong

Constable called his wife 'My dearest Life'.

> 'And this is the wonder that's keeping the stars apart
> I carry your heart, I carry it in my heart.'

The gaiety of love, the sheer fun of it. The gaiety between lovers, between husband and wife, between parents and children, between friends. It is the pleasure of something seen, but unspoken, or spoken by both at once, or spoken by one and catching the other's mood. When my friends die I find I miss them most when I think of a joke they would have liked.

I love private languages. Real intimiacy has only been achieved between human beings when they get to the point of talking mostly in code.

With pain and difficulty we establish our identity as a person, as a man or woman. We are ready to love. Then, in loving, we discover how precarious, how ambiguous, is our personal and sexual identity, as we learn how to play with the boundaries of the self. Eventually we discover the joke, the paradox—the self is only the self when it forgets the boundary. Ecstasy, selfhood, are the moment when we lose the self. 'If a man would follow me, let him deny himself . . .'

There is terror and pain, as well as joy.

The sense of danger must not disappear:
The way is certainly both short and steep,
However gradual it looks from here;
Look if you like, but you will have to leap.
[W. H. Auden]

As we grow older love becomes more diffuse. 'I can love both her and her.' I find myself longing to tell all sorts of people that I love them. And people say it much more to me than in the days when I longed to hear it. When you can say it, and hear it without assuming that love is about possession, it is wonderful how rich all relationships become.

From **The Collected Poems of Stevie Smith**

HUMAN AFFECTION

Mother, I love you so.
Said the child, I love you more than I know.
She laid her head on her mother's arm,
And the love between them kept them warm.

Anonymous, *set to music by* Robert Jones *in* **The Muse's Garden of Delight**

THE FOUNTAINS SMOKE

The fountains smoke, and yet no flames they show;
Stars shine all night, though undiscerned by day;
And trees do spring, yet are not seen to grow;
And shadows move, although they seem to stay.
In winter's woe is buried summer's bliss,
And Love loves most when Love most secret is.

The stillest streams descry the greatest deep;
The clearest sky is subject to a shower;
Conceit's most sweet whenas it seems to sleep;
And fairest days do in the morning lower
The silent groves sweet nymphs they cannot miss,
For Love loves most where Love most secret is.

The rarest jewels hidden virtue yield;
The sweet of traffic is a secret gain;
The year once old doth show a barren field;
And plants seem dead, and yet they spring again:
Cupid is blind: the reason why is this.
Love loveth most when Love most secret is.

From **The Moment of Truth** *by* Ladislaus Boros

MYSTERIUM MORTIS

In order to attain the being-with in love, our own existence must, so to speak, be given up; it must give up making use of the other person and treating him as a possession. Quite simply, man is meant to come to a personal fulfilment. His existence has not yet really come 'to be'; it has first to be created in a community of persons, in the last analysis that means in love; but love means powerlessness.

To love means, of course, to renounce any exercise of power and desire to interfere with, to 'manage', to gain for oneself or to 'possess' any other person. Love leaves the other person free; indeed love creates freedom in the other person; and in this case, creating freedom means self-effacement and renunciation. Love is realized in a great movement of self-emptying and, when once realized, is no more 'our own' love, but comes to us from the other person; it is a pure gift. In this gift and as gift we become what we 'are'; that is, it is as gift that we begin 'to be'. The soul's trusting readiness to surrender itself and be at another's disposal . . . creates the possibility of love and, therefore, of being. In order to be, one must surrender oneself. This is the first basic insight in Marcel's analysis of love.

From **Collected Poems of Kathleen Raine**

AMO ERGO SUM

Because I love
  The sun pours out its rays of living gold
  Pours out its gold and silver on the sea.

Because I love
  The earth upon her astral spindle winds
  Her ecstasy-producing dance.

Because I love
  Clouds travel on the winds through wide skies
  Skies wide and beautiful, blue and deep.

Because I love
  Wind blows white sails,
  The wind blows over flowers, the sweet wind blows.

Because I love
  The ferns grow green, and green the grass, and green
  The transparent sunlit trees.

Because I love
  Larks rise up from the grass
  And all the leaves are full of singing birds.

Because I love
  The summer air quivers with a thousand wings,
  Myriads of jewelled eyes burn in the light.

Because I love
  The iridescent shells upon the sand
  Take forms as fine and intricate as thought.

Because I love
  There is an invisible way across the sky
  Birds travel by that way, the sun and moon
  And all the stars travel that path by night.

Because I love
  There is a river flowing all night long.

Because I love
  All night the river flows into my sleep,
  Ten thousand living things are sleeping in my arms,
  And sleeping wake, and flowing are at rest.

By St Francis of Assisi

LAUDA LXXXI. JACOPONE DA TODI

Love, Thou didst enter very softly in
  To hold this heart of mine.
  No sound, no stir, no sign!
How couldst Thou cross my threshold all unseen?

O sweet and gentle Love, Thou art the key
  Of heaven's city and fort:
  Steer thou my ship to port,
And from the tempest's fury shelter me.

From **The Art of Loving** *by* Eric Fromm

To love means to commit oneself without guarantee, to give oneself completely in the hope that our love will produce love in the loved one. Love is an act of faith, and whatever is of little faith is also of little love.

From **The White Witch** *by* Elizabeth Goudge

The tide of love can play queer tricks, for it never stays still, it is always coming in or going out, but it can come in so slowly that years pass before the one who loves realises that what was at first a thin bright line upon the skyline is now a brimming flood. Or it comes in suddenly like a tidal wave, and breaks in choking brightness over your head before you know where you are.

From **Sheet-Anchor** *by* Eve Stuart

RETURNING TO SEA

Sing, nightingale, and summer birds arise,
To drown the recreant music of farewell—
The midnight dockyard where the blue light lies,
The moment when there is no more to tell,
The long look, and the brave anticipant eyes
While the sea waits, and the dark waters swell.

There will be spring again, the young leaf lent,
The blossom lavished, and the rose revealed,
The calm enormous star, the young bow bent
At evening in the cuckoo-calling field,
The squandered beauty that is never spent
And all the matchless wealth that summers yield.

The spring was ours: sorrow no more to lose
That long abundant summer of the heart;
Should we love's sharp eternity refuse
Because the end crowds in upon the start?
We were alive, we loved, now let us choose
To live as if we never had to part.

To love and to relinquish love's possessing,
To feel the joy more instant than the pain,
All ardours of the greedy heart addressing
Towards that past incomparable gain,
And from the fountain of remembered blessing
To drink the stream and never thirst again.

By Thomas Traherne

O God, who by love alone art great and glorious, that art present and livest with us by love alone: Grant us likewise by love to attain another self, by love to live in others, and by love to come to our glory, to see and accompany Thy love throughout all eternity.

From **Conversations with Kafka** *by* Gustav Janouch

'Youth is full of sunshine and love. Youth is happy, because it has the ability to see beauty. When this ability is lost, wretched old age begins, decay, unhappiness.'

'So age excludes the possibility of happiness?'

'No, happiness excludes age.' Smiling, he bent his head between his hunched shoulders. 'Anyone who keeps the ability to see beauty never grows old.'

LAUGHTER and JOY

'Shall we laugh?'

From **The Complete Poems** *by* Walter de la Mare

But Oh, my dear, how rich and rare, and root-down-
deep and wild and sweet
It is to laugh!

From **No Memory of Crying** *by* Daphne Silver

What do you do with your laughing heart
the day love comes to you?
School it and teach it not to beat,
let it consume you with fiery heat
or go dancing with it down the street,
seeing lifes beauty anew,
feeling a being apart?

What do you do with your crazy dreams
the day love comes to you?
Treat them as delicate, fragile things;
let them fly round your heart on wings
clutching the glory that each one brings
and flinging it into the blue—
watching the way it gleams?

What do you do with your laughing eyes
the day love comes to you?
Revel in all the beauty they know?
Modestly cast them down below
or let them shine so the world may know

what fortune has come to you
from the wide and wondering skies?

From **Prayers of Grief and Glory** *by* Richard Harries

If you were given the job of designing the perfect person I wonder how he would turn out. Suppose for example instead of having to choose ten discs for your lonely desert island you had to choose an ideal companion, what qualities would you pick? I imagine we would all agree that the person must have a sense of humour. It would be terrible to live with someone incapable of laughing or sharing a joke. And this isn't just because people who can laugh with us are fun but because a sense of humour is essential for keeping things in perspective. People who can't laugh usually take themselves too seriously. Then I would want someone with something up top. They wouldn't have to be highly educated but they would have to bc capable of thinking for themselves. We would of course want our companion to be kind but I think we would also agree that there is more to goodness than a warm heart; we would want them to have some steel to them, some guts. We don't want them to go to pieces or collapse in a heap of self-pity.

Then finally a quality that not everyone would value. I would design the ideal companion to be a holy person—a person who had a secret inner life that was deep and close to God. People who are labelled religious usually turn out to be the best or the worst people we know—this is because what is highest in human life can turn out terrible if it is even the slightest bit distorted. But if a person really is close to God they often seem to have a special something that is very attractive and very necessary for that desert island; for after all when you have made yourself comfortable and eaten your coconuts and swum and sunbathed what is your life actually going to be about? A holy person would be a reminder that life is meant to be a spiritual journey into ever deeper layers of truth. That then is my ideal companion—a person capable of laughing, particularly at themselves, able to rub two thoughts together, warm-hearted with a tough core, and finally the quality we wouldn't all agree about, holiness.

From **The Initials in the Heart** *by* Laurence Whistler

Perhaps one could laugh at anything if one was serious about everything. In the grate or in a bonfire, a flame may appear to flicker just above its subject, as if detached and feeding on the air itself. Laughter was like that. Happy when the substance beneath is happiness. For laughter itself is not happiness. It may, as everyone knows, conceal a void like an ache.

From an article by Lionel Blue in **Contact**

HUMOUR IN RELIGION

The grace of humour should not be underrated—for grace it is. It has helped Jews transform their own bitterness. In Jewish jokes about Hitler for example, he always comes over as a figure of fun, not as a portent or horror. A great deal of life is tragedy, and suffering is woven into it. A lot of it cannot be changed—it is part and parcel of what we are and the world we live in. The only thing we can change is our attitude to it. The same event can be regarded as tragic, farce, or comic. Judaism assimilates tragedy by refusing to accept it on its own terms. . . . We have to protect our souls from our hate and bitterness, and that is real, not an exercise in ecumenism.

From **An Anatomy of Laughter** *by* Richard Boston

We need laughter, just as we need love. Were we entirely rational without any hang-ups, neuroses or tensions, then we would need neither. Laughter is like the pearl which the oyster forms around a speck of irritation. The entirely healthy oyster produces no pearls and the inhabitants of Utopia (like Jesus) do not laugh. Laughter exists in an imperfect world, and it makes us rejoice that it *is* imperfect. Sydney Smith, who was right about so many things, was right about this.

Man could direct his ways by plain reason, and support his life by tasteless food; but God has given us wit, and flavour, and brightness, and laughter, and perfumes, to enliven the days of man's pilgrimage, and to 'charm his pained steps over the burning marle'.

From **Songs of Innocence** *by* William Blake

Piping down the valleys wild,
Piping songs of pleasant glee,
On a cloud I saw a child,
And he laughing said to me:

'Pipe a song about a Lamb!'
So I piped with merry cheer.
'Piper, pipe that song again;'
So I piped: he wept to hear.

'Drop thy pipe, thy happy pipe,
Sing thy songs of happy cheer.'
So I sung the same again,
While he wept with joy to hear.

'Piper, sit thee down and write
In a book that all may read.'
So he vanished from my sight;
And I plucked a hollow reed.

And I made a rural pen,
And I stain'd the water clear,
And I wrote my happy songs
Every child may joy to hear.

From **The Dyer's Hand** *by* W. H. Auden

NOTES ON THE COMIC

Among those whom I like and admire, I can find no common denominator but among those whom I love, I can: all of them make me laugh.

From **Tensions** *by* H. A. Williams

THE DELECTABLE MOUNTAINS

If people catch a glimpse of their conflicts resolved, what is the universal form of that vision?

I suggest that it is laughter.

I mean real laughter at what is seen as inherently funny. What is the test of real laughter? It is the ability to see the funny side of your own situation, the ability to laugh at yourself as well as about other people. Without the ability to laugh at yourself, to find delighted pleasure in the comic aspects of your own character and circumstances, laughter becomes perverted: a superior sneer, a transparent disguise for cynicism and defeat, a defence mechanism to give to others and yourself the impression that you are more at ease and less frightened than in fact you are—committee laughter, cocktail-party laughter, self-consciously Christian laughter: 'We may be dead but by God we can be cheerful.' A man who laughs at himself, who enjoys the fun of being what he is, does not fall into the perversion of laughter. Mirth, like charity, has to begin at home if it is to be genuine.

In one of Christopher Fry's plays an ageing couple talk of decay and mortality. 'Shall we laugh?' asks the man. 'For what reason?' asks the woman. 'For the reason of laughter,' is the reply, 'since laughter is surely the surest touch of genius in creation. Would *you* ever have thought of it? That same laughter, madam, is an irrelevancy which almost amounts to revelation.'

God, we believe, accepts us, accepts all men, unconditionally, warts and all. Laughter is the purest form of our response to God's acceptance of us. For when I laugh at myself I accept myself and when I laugh at other people in genuine mirth I accept them. Self-acceptance in laughter is the very opposite of self-satisfaction or pride. For in laughter I accept myself not because I'm some sort of super-person, but precisely because I'm not. There is nothing funny about a super-person. There is everything funny about a man who thinks he is. In laughing at my own claims to importance or regard I receive myself in a sort of loving forgiveness which is an echo of God's forgiveness of me. In much conventional contrition there is a selfishness and pride which are scarcely hidden. In our desperate self-concern we blame ourselves for not being the super-persons we think we really are. But in laughter we sit light to ourselves. That is why laughter is the purest form of our response to God.

. . . So, from the bottom of your heart thank God when you can see the joke popping out of your circumstances, even when they are grim. Thank God when you can take a delighted pleasure in the comic spectacle which is yourself, especially if it is yourself devoutly at prayer. (Why am I like a famous jackdaw?) Thank God when you can laugh. It means that you are on the Delectable Mountains and that your redemption has drawn nigh.

From **Queen Lucia** *by* E. F. Benson

THE MEDITATION GROUP

It was quite clear at the class this morning that though the pupils were quite interested in the abstract messages of love which they were about to shoot out in all directions, and in the atmosphere of peace with which they were to surround themselves, the branch of the subject which thrilled them to the marrow was the breathing exercises and contortions which, if persevered with, would give them youth and activity, faultless digestions and indefatigable energy. They all sat on the floor, and stopped up alternate nostrils, and held their breath till Mrs Quantock got purple in the face, and Georgie and Lucia red, and expelled their breath again, either with sudden puffs which set the rushes on the floor quivering, or with long, quiet exhalations. Then there were certain postures to be learned, in one of which, entailing the bending of the body forward, two of Georgie's trouser-buttons gave way with a sharp snap, and he felt the corresponding member of his braces, thus violently released, spring up to his shoulder. Various other embarrassing noises issued from Lucia and Daisy that sounded like the bursting of strings or tapes, but everybody pretended to hear nothing at all, or covered up the report of the explosion with coughings and clearing of the throat. But apart from these discordances, everything was fairly harmonious.

. . . At the end Lucia, with her far-away look, emerged, you might say, in a dazed condition from the fastnesses of Tibet, where they had been in communion with the Guides, whose wisdom the Guru interpreted to them.

From **Creative Unity** *by* Rabindranath Tagore

And joy is everywhere; it is in the earth's green covering of grass: in the blue serenity of the sky; in the reckless exuberance of spring; in the severe abstinence of grey winter; in the living flesh that animates our bodily frame; in the perfect poise of the human figure, noble and upright; in living; in the exercise of all our powers; in the acquisition of knowledge; in fighting evils; in dying for gains we never can share. Joy is there everywhere; it is superfluous, unnecessary, nay, it very often contradicts the most peremptory behests of necessity. It exists to show that the bonds of love can only be explained by love; they are like body and soul. Joy is the realisation of the truth of oneness, the oneness of our soul with the world and of the world-soul with the supreme lover.

Prayer

O God the source of the whole world's gladness and bearer of its pain
May your unconquerable joy rest at the heart of all our trouble and distress, through Jesus Christ our Lord and Saviour. Amen.

In thinking about living and loving, it is impossible to omit the fact of suffering, it would be like living in a fool's paradise were we to do so, but I think C. S. Lewis *has a lot to say about the possible reason for at least the insecurity of life.*

The Christian doctrine of suffering explains, I believe, a very curious fact about the world we live in. The settled happiness and security which we all desire, God withholds from us by the very nature of the world: but joy, pleasure and merriment, He has scattered broadcast. We are never safe, but we have plenty of fun, and some ecstasy. It is not hard to see why. The security we crave would teach us to rest our hearts in this world and oppose an obstacle to our return to God: a few moments of happy love, a landscape, a symphony, a merry meeting with our friends, have no such tendency—Our Father refreshes us on the journey with some pleasant inns, but will not encourage us to mistake them for home.

From **Poems** *by* John Masefield

LAUGH AND BE MERRY

Laugh and be merry, remember, better the world with a song,
Better the world with a blow in the teeth of a wrong.
Laugh, for the time is brief, a thread the length of a span.
Laugh and be proud to belong to the old proud pageant of man.
Laugh and be merry: remember, in olden time,
God made heaven and earth for joy He took in a rhyme,
Made them, and filled them full with the strong red wine of His mirth,
The splendid joy of the stars: the joy of the earth.
So we must laugh and drink from the deep blue cup of the sky,
Join the jubilant song of the great stars sweeping by,
Laugh, and battle, and work, and drink of the wine outpoured
In the dear green earth, the sign of the joy of the Lord.
Laugh and be merry together, like brothers akin,
Guesting awhile in the rooms of a beautiful inn,
Glad till the dancing stops, and the lilt of music ends.
Laugh till the game is played; and be you merry, my friends.

By King George VI, BBC Radio Broadcast, 15 August 1945

For merriment is the birthright of the young. But we can all keep it in our hearts as life goes on if we hold fast by the spirit that refuses to admit defeat; by the faith that never falters; by the hope that cannot be quenched.

From an article in the Parish Magazine of All Saints, Worlingham.

WHY THE FLOOD CAME

And the Lord said unto Noah, 'Where is the Ark which I have commanded thee to build?'

And Noah said unto the Lord: 'Verily, I have had three carpenters off ill. The supplier of gopher wood hath let me down—yes even though the gopher wood hath been on order for nigh on twelve months. The Damp Course specialist hath not turned up—what can I do, O Lord?'

And God said unto Noah, 'I want that Ark finished even after seven days and seven nights.'

And Noah said: 'It will be so.' And it was *not* so. . . . Again, the Lord said unto Noah, 'What seemeth to be the trouble this time?'

And Noah said unto the Lord: 'Mine subcontractor hath gone bankrupt. The pitch which Thou commandest me to put on the outside and on the inside of the ark hath not arrived. The plumber hath gone on strike.'

Then Noah rent his garments and continued: 'The glazier departeth on a holiday to Majorca—yea even though I offereth him Double Time. Shem, my son who helpeth me on the ark side of the business, hath formed a pop group with his brothers Ham and Japheth . . . Lord, I am undone.'

And lo it was not fulfilled.

Then Noah said unto the Lord: 'The gopher wood supplier waiteth only on his servant to find the invoices before he delivereth the wood unto me.'

And the Lord grew angry and said: 'What about the animals? Of fowls of the air after their kind, and of every creeping thing of the Earth after his kind—two of every sort have I ordered to come unto thee, to keep them alive. Where, for example, are the giraffes?' And Noah said unto the Lord: 'They are expected today.'

Again, the Lord said unto Noah: 'And where are the clean beasts both male and female, to keep their seed alive on the face of the Earth?'

And Noah said: 'The van cometh on Tuesday: yea and yea, it will be so.'

And the Lord said unto Noah: 'How about the unicorns?'

Then Noah wrung his hands and wept, saying: 'Lord, Lord they are a discontinued line. Thou canst not get unicorns for love nor money, any more.'

And God said, 'Where are the monkeys, the bears, the hippopotami and the elephants, the Zebras and the hartebeasts, two of each kind and of the fowls of the air by sevens, both male and female?'

And Noah replied unto the Lord: 'They have been delivered to the wrong address—but should arrive on Friday: All save the fowls of the air by sevens. For it has just been told me that the fowls of the air are sold only in half dozens.'

Whereupon Noah kissed the Earth and said: 'Lord, Lord, Thou knowest in Thy wisdom, what it is like with delivery dates.'

And the Lord, in his wisdom, made reply: 'Noah My son, I knowest. Why else dost thou think I have caused a Flood to descend upon all the Earth?'

From **The Gentleman in Row D** *by* Virginia Graham

Dear Sir, we in row D are well aware
Your soul is steeped in music to the core.
You love, we notice, each succeeding air
More deeply than the one which came before.

You lead the orchestra in perfect time,
With ever-nodding head you set the pace,
We in Row D consider it a crime
You are not in Sir Thomas Beecham's place.

Your lily hands most delicately haver,
Each phrase is ended with a graceful twist,
You know, it seems, each breve and semi-quaver,
And play them gently on your other wrist.

Sometimes you hum the least familiar portions,
And beat upon the floor a faint tattoo,
Though we can stand a lot of your contortions,
We shouldn't tap too much if we were you.

Dear Sir, we need no musical instructor,
We also sang in oratorio,
And if you were a really good conductor,
Our lightning would have struck you hours ago!

From **Gitanjali** *by* Rabindranath Tagore

LVII

Light, my light, the world-filling light, the eye-kissing light, heart-sweetening light!

Ah; the light dances, my darling, at the centre of my life; the light strikes, my darling, the chords of my love; the sky opens, the wind runs wild, laughter passes over the earth.

The butterflies spread their sails on the sea of light. Lilies and jasmines surge up on the crest of the waves of light.

The light is shattered into gold on every cloud, my darling, and it scatters gems in profusion.

Mirth spreads from leaf to leaf, my darling, and gladness without measure. The heaven's river has drowned its banks and the flood of joy is abroad.

From **Prayers of Hope** *by* Richard Harries

O God grant that we may both see the truth and see it with a merciful eye.

That we may laugh and make others laugh and be led beyond laughter to you in whom truth and mercy meet together.

Part III

LOOKING and LISTENING

THE ARTIST

THE DANCER

THE SCULPTOR

THE MUSICIAN

THE POET

LOOKING and LISTENING

'So that You can hear me'

From **Towards Democracy** *by* Edward Carpenter

Lo! the rippling stream and the stars and the naked tree branches deliver themselves up to him. They come close; they are his body, and his spirit is rapt among them: without thought he hears what they and all things would say.

By E. B.

LOVE IS THE BRIDGE

If 'love is life coupling together the lover and the loved' as Richard Rollé has said, then surely that love is the bridge which links God to man and man to God, and the samc bridge which spans the gap in every possible human situation: in the words of the well-known song 'A Bridge Over Troubled Waters', the bridge of communication, the bridge connecting the space with the object, the bridge of love which holds the world together.

I suspect that the source of most of our troubles today is the inability to communicate with each other, person to person. On every side we see the misery caused by misunderstanding and lack of trust. So often it snowballs into hatred and violence and non-co-operation at every level, between husband and wife and parents and children, between management and the shop floor, between nations, and people with different skin colours, cultures and faiths, and finally results in the alienation of man from God his creator.

Perhaps the answer lies in learning to listen to what the other is trying to say, to listen with the whole of our attention in silence and sympathy.

O Lord, open our eyes that we may see and our ears that we may hear; open our minds and our hearts that when we are with someone who is finding his cross hard to bear we may be able to let the holy Spirit speak through us bringing him comfort and hope. And this we ask for Jesus Christ's sake, and in his Name. Amen.

From **Prayer for the Day,** BBC Radio, *by* Michael Mayne

Jesus had a lot to say about seeing, about blind eyes and deaf ears. 'Have you no perception?' he asked his disciples. 'Have you eyes that do not see, ears that do not hear?' For of course there is a seeing with the eyes and what has sometimes been described as a seeing with the heart. In the book by St Exupéry called *The Little Prince*, the little prince says: 'In your world, men cultivate five thousand roses in one garden and still they do not find what they seek. And yet what they are seeking may be found in a single rose or a drop of water . . . but the eyes are blind: one must seek with the heart.'

A seeking—and a seeing—with the heart. A seeing beneath the surface so that things and people begin to be glimpsed as they truly are. That will mean looking at each other and seeing a unique and miraculous complex of flesh and spirit made in God's likeness and created for eternal life. It will mean looking at the tree, the rose, the drop of water and seeing God's presence everywhere in his world. These are mysteries which should reduce us to silence because we are fearful of the majesty of a God who creates from nothing a world of such surpassing wonder.

Lord, teach me today to be still, so that I may begin to see signs of your presence all about me all the time. Amen.

From **A Grief Observed** *by* C. S. Lewis

To see, in some measure, like God. His love and His knowledge are not distinct from one another, nor from Him.

We could almost say He sees because He loves, and therefore loves although He sees.

From **Prayer for the Day,** BBC Radio, *by* Michael Mayne

Learning to be still in order to listen. Learning to be still in order to see. Learning to create a space at the centre of your being where you are open to the Spirit of God.

. . . William Blake once wrote: 'The tree which moves some to tears of joy is in the eyes of others only a green thing which stands in the way.' If I am to become sensitive to God I must begin by becoming sensitive to his world: seeing it with the clear and wondering eyes of a child.

Whether a tree is just a lump of wood standing in my way or something that can reduce me to the silence of awe and wonder depends on whether, like Gerard Manley Hopkins, I believe that 'the world *is* charged with the grandeur of God'; that despite all its pain and anguish it's not simply beautiful but sacramental; that if I have learned to look at it aright then every part of the creation *can* reveal God to me. The novelist Patrick White puts on the fly-leaf of one of his books the couplet:

There is another world
But it is in this one.

The very familiarity of the world about us serves as a kind of cataract which blinds us to the sheer prodigality of a God whose world of colours and sights and sounds ought to make us drunk with their beauty. And time and time again it is the artist—the poet, the painter, the musician, the novelist—who sees beneath the surface of things to that deeper dimension of spirit, and by their choice of words or notes of music, or their use of paint or wood or stone, capture a truth about the mystery and wonder of life which causes us to catch our breath as for a moment we see with their eyes and share their vision.

By Pablo Neruda, *quoted in* **Jesus Ahead** *by* Gerard Bessiere

POEM

So that you can hear me
At times
My words get fainter and fainter,
Like the marks made by seagulls on the sand.

From **The Go-Between God** *by* John V. Taylor

The Holy Spirit is that power which opens eyes that are closed, hearts that are unaware and minds that shrink from too much reality. If one is open towards God, one is open also to the beauty of the world, the truth of ideas, and the pain of disappointment and deformity. If one is closed up against being hurt, or blind towards one's fellow-men, one is inevitably shut off from God also. One cannot choose to be open in one direction and closed in another. Vision and vulnerability go together. Insensitivity also is an all-rounder. If for one reason or another we refuse really to *see* another person, we become incapable of sensing the presence of God.

The spirit of man is that facility which enables each of us to be truly present to another. The Spirit of God is that power of communion which enables every other reality, and the God who is within and behind all realities, to be present to us.

From **The Collected Poems of Stevie Smith**

NOT WAVING BUT DROWNING

Nobody heard him, the dead man,
But still he lay moaning:
I was much further out than you thought
And not waving but drowning.

Poor chap, he always loved larking
And now he's dead
It must have been too cold for him his heart gave way,
They said.

Oh, no no no, it was too cold always
(Still the dead one lay moaning)
I was much too far out all my life
And not waving but drowning.

Anonymous

My compassion is an ever welling spring
Flowing through you.

From **The Go-Between God** *by* John V. Taylor

In these days more and more people are sick and lost because they do not know with any certainty who they are or what they are. They can find their identity and their role only when someone else sees them with love. It is useless to call for repentence or commitment until we have first given acceptance. No one can change until he can first of all *be*. No one can give himself until he has a self to give.

. . . 'I would know my shadow and my light, so shall I at last be whole.' (The child of our times.)

From **Thought for the Day**, BBC Radio, *by* Michael Marshall

It is only when Beauty puts her loving arms round the Beast that he is transformed into the Prince of her dreams.

From **Longing and Listening** *by* E. B., BBC Radio 'Epilogue'

Not longing only, but listening also. There is a great need today for hearts that listen.

Martin Israel assures us that we do not have to rely upon ourselves alone when trying to solve the problems with which we are confronted. He says,

'When we are able to listen in silence to the life story of another person and not respond with our own wisdom, a greater wisdom, that of the Holy Spirit who is the Advocate, will flow from our lips and will lead both that other person and ourselves into the truth. From the lips of silence proceeds wisdom the Word of God, from the hushed heart flows love.'

Anonymous, *heard on the radio*

By listening it is possible to bring a man's soul into being.

From The Collected Poems of Edwin Muir

THE HEART COULD NEVER SPEAK

The heart could never speak
But that the Word was spoken.
We hear the heart break
Here with hearts unbroken.
Time, teach us the art
That breaks and heals the heart.

Heart, you would be dumb
But that your word was said
In time, and the echoes come
Thronging from the dead.
Time, teach us the art
That resurrects the heart.

Tongue, you can only say
Syllables, joy and pain,
Till time, having its way,
Makes the word live again.
Time, merciful lord,
Grant us to learn your word.

By Pedro Salinas, *quoted in* **Jesus Ahead** *by* Gerard Bessiere

POEM

I look for you
behind people.
Not in your name—if they say it.
Not in your image—if they paint it.
Behind, behind, beyond.
I look behind and beyond you.

From **Fruits of Silence** *by* Hugh L'Anson Fausset

How seldom do we understand each other despite all the words we barter. Yet it is well known that those who are well attuned can often communicate without words or merely by verbal hints because they are near to each other in the silence of the mind.

This silence of the mind makes possible a new relationship of immediate perception. We discover that beneath the external surface of the mind is a realm of consciousness which contains our individual minds and unites them. Here, in this wordless region of immediate awareness, we are not shut off from each other by our own private mental world, with its interests and prejudices . . . Mind here is as vast, all inclusive and penetrating as space, and every expression of thought springs from this unexpressed source. When we are in union with it, we are in union with the essence of every other mind, however it may differ in its mental habits or outlook.

This silent region of the mind is also a silence of the heart. For in the deeper and higher consciousness heart and mind are undivided. When we are in rapport with it we understand by sympathy and identification. This does not prevent us from perceiving error or confusion where they exist in someone's reasoning. But we see beneath these the truth that is struggling to find utterance, and where the expression is inadequate, we yet grasp the meaning. For we are in touch with what is unexpressed in the speaker's mind as it is in our own.

. . . To discover the Silence, then, in solitary meditation is to establish a relationship with our creative source which transforms our relations with the whole of objective existence, with the natural world and our fellow-beings. In it we are weaned from that attachment to ourselves and to the phenomenal world which prevents us from living imaginatively.

This weaning is, of course, accomplished in us in other ways than in the stillness and emptiness of solitary mediation. For the way to reality is in every situation which encourages or compels us to commit ourselves to life more fundamentally. It offers itself to us in the testings of personal tragedy or frustration, in times when we can only patiently suffer and endure, and in the opportunities of devoted service or of dedication, to a work which demands all we have to give in courage, insight and skill. Indeed there is no situation however apparently discouraging or unbearable or however joyous and uplifting, in which we cannot learn to participate in life more deeply, to respond more finely to the spirit's hidden directives, to love more sensitively and relate ourselves more intelligently to the genius of truth in all that is.

From **The White Snow of Meditation** *by* Clare Cameron, *with acknowledgement to* Chu Chan

Be very still before this beauty
That nothing asks of you.
Let not the wind of thought arise.
Or the sunlight of your worship.
Make no track upon it with eager footsteps.
Be very still before this beauty.
Offering in silence the landscape of your heart
To the falling of the snow.

From **The Night Sky of the Lord** *by* Alan Ecclestone

There are things that can only be seen in darkened skies, questions only heard in the silence of utter dismay. Such a time is ours. We are poised at a moment in history when the madness of mere seconds could unloose upon the world a frenzied self-destruction such as no generation before could have conceived. This is the moment in which the questions put to the Jews may, if heard, and answered with fear and trembling yet with trust and hope, be the way of man's salvation. To whom else shall we go? Jew and Christian alike, Jew and non-Jew, may find in Him who they have all in their various ways rejected, despised, spat upon and mocked, their one hope of life for mankind. The furnaces of Auschwitz in which Jewish victims perished may be the fires in which the heart of mankind must be purged anew.

By T. E. Brown, *quoted in* **A Vision of the Aquarian Age** *by* George Trevelyan

THE SHELL

If thou coulds't empty all thyself of self
Like to a shell dishabited
Then might He find thee on an ocean shelf
And say: 'This is not dead'
And fill thee with Himself instead.

But thou art so replete with very thou
And hast such shrewd activity
That when He comes He'll say 'It is enow
Unto itself—'twere better let it be:
It is so small and full
And has no need of Me'.

THE ARTIST

'The bridge which leads from the visible to the invisible'

From **Markings** *by* Dag Hammarskjöld

Thou takest the pen—and the lines dance. Thou takest the flute—and the notes shimmer. Thou takest the brush—and the colours sing. So all things have meaning and beauty in that space beyond time where Thou art. How then can I hold back anything from Thee?

From **Painting As a Pastime** *by* Winston Churchill

Happy are the painters for they shall not be lonely. Light and colour, peace and hope will keep them company to the end, or almost to the end, of the day.

From **On My Painting** *by* Max Beckmann, *in* **Modern Artists on Art**

What I want to show in my work is the idea which hides itself behind so-called reality. I am seeking for the bridge which leads from the visible to the invisible, like the famous cabalist who once said: 'If you wish to get hold of the invisible you must penetrate as deeply as possible into the visible.'

My aim is always to get hold of the magic of reality and to transfer this reality into painting—to make the invisible visible through reality. It may sound paradoxical, but it is, in fact, reality which forms the mystery of our existence.

What helps me most in this task is the penetration of space.

Height, width, and depth are the three phenomena which I must transfer into one plane to form the abstract surface of the picture, and thus to protect myself from the infinity of space. My figures come and go, suggested by fortune or misfortune. I try to fix them divested of their apparent accidental quality.

One of my problems is to find the Self, which has only one form and is immortal—to find it in animals and men, in the heaven and in the hell which together form the world in which we live.

Space, and space again, is the infinite deity which surrounds us and in which we are ourselves contained.

That is what I try to express through painting, a function different from poetry and music, but for me predestined necessity.

From **The Spirit In Man, Art, and Literature**
by C. G. Jung

A great work of art is like a dream; for all its apparent obviousness it does not explain itself and is always ambiguous. A dream never says 'you ought' or 'this is the truth.' It presents an image in much the same way as nature allows a plant to grow, and it is up to us to draw conclusions. If a person has a nightmare, it means he is either too much given to fear, or too exempt from it; if he dreams of a wise old man, it means he is either too much of a pedant or else in need of a teacher. In a subtle way both meanings come to the same thing, as we realize when we let a work of art act upon us as it acted upon the artist. To grasp its meaning, we must allow it to shape us as it shaped him. Then we also understand the nature of his primordial experience. He has plunged into the healing and redeeming depths of the collective psyche, where man is not lost in the isolation of consciousness and its errors and sufferings, but where all men are caught in a common rhythm which allows the individual to communicate his feelings and strivings to mankind as a whole.

This re-immersion in the state of *participation mystique* is the secret of artistic creation and of the effect which great art has upon us, for at that level of experience it is no longer the weal or woe of the individual that counts, but the life of the collective. That is why every great work of art is objective and impersonal, and yet profoundly moving. And that is also why the personal life of the artist is at most a help or a hindrance, but is never essential to his creative task. He may go the way of the Philistine, a good citizen, a fool, or a criminal. His personal career may be interesting and inevitable, but it does not explain his art.

From **Revelation: Letters Written From the Other Side of Death**

LITERATURE, POETRY AND ART

You have to be sure that all the time and pains you spend in the world are expended on the things that belong to eternity.

Art, beauty, music, literature are all the products of the soul and can go on for ever.

We remember and rejoice in all the lovely things we saw and heard on earth and we have got a spiritual version of them here.

It is so funny to come across a picture that you have always loved and to see not the picture itself but the meaning of it.

Pictures if they are worth anything at all, are not just the faithful representations of anything material, they are the effort of someone, who has vision into the things of the spirit, to interpret them to other people by means of form and colour.

When someone who is a real artist sits down to paint a picture he should not be thinking of depicting the thing as it is, but as it should be if it were setting forth the glory of God.

The landscape painter is not just painting hills and snow and earth and material trees, or even material flowers. He is painting height, purity, space, the glorious freshness of the spring, the riot of colour which the flowers convey to our minds, and thus has a message to give which conveys something above the actual sight, which raises the thoughts of people above material things.

From **The Daily Office**

Give us growing reverence for the truth and such wisdom
in the use of knowledge,
That your kingdom may be advanced and your
name glorified
Through Jesus Christ our Lord. Amen.

From **Human Bridges** *by* Steven Ratiner

All art is bridge building—a movement from the mind's horizon over into the shared world, from apprehended thoughts into solid creations. . . . As in our own world there is a constant potential for the heart's release, the heart's crossing. When we approach the world with open eyes and a measure of wonder, it is our own clarity that completes the arc.

From **Dear Theo: An Autobiography of Vincent Van Gogh From His Letters,** *edited by* Irving Stone

Oh, my dear Theo, if you could see the olive groves just now! The leaves like old silver, and silver turning to green against the blue, and the orange-coloured ploughed earth. It is something quite different from your idea of it in the North. It is like the pollard willows of our Dutch meadows or the oak bushes of our dunes; the rustle of an olive grove has something very secret in it, and immensely old. It is too beautiful for us to dare to paint it or to be able to imagine it.

The figure of a labourer—some furrows in a ploughed field—a bit of sand, sea and sky—are serious subjects, so difficult, but at the same time so beautiful, that it is indeed worth while to devote one's life to the task of expressing the poetry hidden in them.

From **The Man Who Loved the Sun: The Life of Vincent Van Gogh** *by* Jack Raymond Jones

People to Vincent were always more important than things! 'I would rather paint the eyes of men than cathedrals because in people's eyes there is something that is absent in cathedrals even if they are majestic . . . the soul of a human being, even if it is that of a poor beggar or a street woman, is to my eycs more interesting.'

. . .'To know how to suffer without complaining', Van Gogh wrote to Theo, 'is the only practical thing . . . the lesson to be learned, the solution to the problem of life.'

From **Artists On Art,** *compiled and edited by* Robert Goldwater and Marco Treves

JEAN-FRANCOIS MILLET TO THÉOPHILE THORE

In the *Woman Going To Draw Water* I tried to show that she was not a water-carrier or even a servant, but a woman going to draw water for the house, for soup, for her husband and children; that she should not seem to be carrying any greater or less weight than the buckets fill; that under the sort of grimace which the weight on her shoulders causes, and the closing of the eyes at the sunlight, one should see a kind of homely goodness. I have avoided (as I always do with horror) anything that might verge on the sentimental. I wanted her to do her work good-naturedly and simply—as if it were a part of her daily labour, the habit of her life. I wanted to show the coolness of the well, and its antique form is meant to suggest that many before her had come there to draw water.

. . . The gossip about my *Man With a Hoe*, seems to me all very strange. . . . Is it impossible to admit that one can have some sort of idea in seeing a man devoted to gaining his bread by the sweat of his brow? Some tell me that I deny the charms of the country. I find much more than charms—I find infinite glories. I see as well as they do the little flowers of which Christ said that Solomon in all his glory, was not arrayed like one of these. I see the halos of dandelions, and the sun, also, which spreads out beyond the world its glory in the clouds. But I see as well, in the plain, the steaming horses at work, and in a rocky place a man, all worn out, whose 'han' has been heard since morning, and who tries to straighten himself a moment and breathe. The drama is surrounded by beauty.

It is not my invention. This 'cry of the ground' was heard long ago. My critics are men of taste and education, but I cannot put myself in their shoes, and as I have never seen anything but fields since I was born, I try to say as best I can what I saw and felt when I was at work. Those who want to do better have, I'm sure, full chance.

THE DANCER

'An outward and visible sign of an inward and spiritual grace'

By Poppea Vanda, *quoted in* **The Sleeping Ballerina** *by* Anton Dolin

A TRIBUTE TO OLGA SPESSIVTZEVA

Her dancing was an act of faith and had the exquisite beauty of certain God-made things; the sparsely budding black-thorn; the almost luminous haze of the willow in very early spring; a moonlit silver-birch sapling lightly powered with snow. She looked as fragile as an ice-crystal; as insubstantial as vapour. When she danced she was unearthly and entirely whisht; and the quality of beauty she produced caused the heart to miss a beat. She danced, not for herself, not for an audience, but for the Dance itself. Her technique was impeccable and utterly effortless; she never 'faked', and a calm, glowing integrity informed all she did.

Her serenely devotional approach to her work made one feel humble. I never saw her, I never remember her without recalling one of the responses from the Catechism: 'An outward and visible sign of an inward and spiritual grace.'

From **Poems** *by* John Masefield

BALLET RUSSE

The gnome from moonland plays the Chopin air,
The ballerina glides out of the wings,
Like all the Aprils of forgotten Springs.
Smiling she comes, all smile,
All grace; forget the cruel world awhile;
Forget vexation now and sorrow due.
A blue cap sits coquettish in her hair.

She is all youth, all beauty, all delight,
All that a boyhood loves and manhood needs.
What if an Empire perishes, who heeds?
Smiling she comes, her smile
Is all that may inspire, or beguile.
All that our haggard folly thinks untrue.
Upon the trouble of the moonlit strain
She moves like living mercy bringing light.

Soon when the gnomish fingers cease to stray,
She will be gone, still smiling, to the wings,
To live among our unforgotten things,
Centaur and unicorn,
The queens in Avalon and Roland's horn,
The mystery, the magic and the dew
Of a tomorrow and a yesterday.

From **Gitanjali** *by* Rabindranath Tagore

LXIX

The same stream of life that runs through my veins night and day runs through the world and dances in rhythmic measures.

It is the same life that shoots in joy through the dust of the earth in numberless blades of grass and breaks into tumultuous waves of leaves and flowers.

It is the same life that is rocked in the ocean-cradle of birth and of death, in ebb and in flow.

I feel my limbs are made glorious by the touch of this world of life. And my pride is from the life-throb of ages dancing in my blood this moment.

From **No Memory of Crying** *by* Daphne Silver

SWAN LAKE

The curtains lifted slowly, red velvet folds pleating
gracefully upwards with old fashioned elegance.
The stark, blank canvas of the stage quivered
and was still.

Pure liquid notes hung like brilliants in the expectant air
then danced as snowflakes; filigree patterned
in the waiting dark.
The dancer waited, unwilling to mar the perfect emptiness,
then sprang to life and with his body, drew
the outline of the painting carefully.
An arm reached out, gestured—and a willow tree
stood weeping at the lakes' edge, in the wind.
He leapt then stooped, an arrow high into
the snow filled air.
A young swan fluttered down, with damaged wing, to mourn.
With talking feet and speaking hands; with young expressive faces
the dancers painted their exquisite living
picture of a fairy tale—shading the shadows with a sigh—
adding the highlights with a smile.
The once blank canvas now one living scene of colour,
telling of young love—lost love—
love without end.
One final leap, lift and turn and then the dancers stood
eyes, arms and hearts entwined
and signed their lovely painting with a kiss.
Whilst slowly darkening down, red velvet curtains
swished and swept—my earthbound soul—
which, for a little time had danced with them,
crept quietly behind my eyes again—and wept.

From **The Magic of Dance** *by* Margot Fonteyn

NUREYEV

As he makes his entrance, all eyes are riveted on the tiger walking with such dignity and grace to centre stage, looking very concentrated within himself. He makes the preparation for his 'variation' or solo with utmost care and accuracy, and leaps into the air as though pouncing at a prey three times his size. The variation lasts one minute or one minute and a half, the tiger seems to fly above the heads of the corps de ballet, he finishes with a final thrust and holds his pose with an air of victory over dark forces that might have killed him. His breathtaking steps have looked sometimes as easy as a bird flying, sometimes dangerously impossible. The audience has lived through the experience with him.

That is the excitement and the magic of Nureyev.

From **Collected Poems** *by* Frances Cornford

FOR NIJINSKY'S TOMB

Nijinsky's ashes here in peace repose
No more the Faun, the Harlequin, the Rose.

We saw him framed in light before the crowds,
Hushed like a tree that waits the touch of dawn,
A panther ready, or an arrow drawn.
Then music came, the sure, awakening bars,
He leapt beyond the bounds of joy and grief;
His heart conferred in those transfigured hours,
Strength like the sun, precision like the stars;
The sea was his; the buoyancy of clouds,
The sap that flows in every fluted leaf,
The blossoming in light, of fields of flowers.
Yet later, smiling in applauded grace,
The Faun, the Rose was never wholly ours,
We saw the remoteness in the tilted face,
He heard alone, beyond our human ears,
Beyond applause, the Music of the Spheres.

Nijinsky's ashes here in peace are laid
Their perfect tribute to Perfection paid.

From **A Mantis Carol** *by* Laurens van der Post

THE BUSHMEN

Yes they loved dancing so much that they had a dance for everything. Where their words, stories and painting failed them their dancing took over. It was almost as if they knew how the great unknown and imponderables of their lives had to be acted out, to be lived fully to the end in a way for which the dancing was sponsor before it could be known and another great fragment of universal mystery transformed into loving wonder. So they danced as perhaps only the stars and Shiva danced at the heart of the stillness of the darkness to shake it into light.

Of course it was not the dancing you see at the Bolshoi, Covent Garden or the City Ballet of New York, but for me, who's seen dancing at all these places, it was far more moving. He would dance, for instance, the story of man's search for fire and his sense of liberation, gratitude and reverence when with the help of Mantis he found his fire at last. He would dance his joy at the birth of a child and his anguish at the death of a friend. He would dance out his gratitude to the animal his hunter had brought home for having been so good to allow itself to be killed so that he could continue to live. There was nothing he did not have a dance for. It was amazing that as he danced, usually only in the darkest hour of the night, the act that he was dancing conveyed itself to all nature around him not only compelling it to recognize the rhythm but also to become party to it.

I remember for instance a night when they danced their great fire dance and how, as the dance approached its climax towards midnight, the lions began to roar as I've never heard them before, almost as if keeping time with the stamping, dancing feet which made the desert reverberate like a drum, and harmonizing like great bass accompanists, with the voices of the women singing to keep their men dancing, and the sound rising clear, bright and lofty as the highest of the stars. In the end all of desert nature was drawn in, ostriches with their booming, night plovers with their deep-sea piping, owls with their solemn hooting and the night jar with its castanet voices. And in the gaps between the waves of the swelling tide of sound, the night cicada sopranos could be heard like rows of seraphim and cherubim piled on top of one another, their song soaring until it seemed to me it reached high enough to stir the stars themselves and make them to succumb to the rhythm below and go tap dancing all over the shining black floor of that desert heaven. In the end the dancing produced such an atmosphere of oneness and belonging between all that when the climax came and the fire was found I felt that I, who had come so far from so remote a world, was no longer a stranger, standing alone and isolated but someone who had found sanctuary in an ancient temple participating for the first time in an act of natural communion with one of the greatest congregations of life ever gathered.

From **One Hundred Poems of Kabir,** *translated by* Rabindranath Tagore

Dance, my heart: dance
  to-day with joy!
The strains of love fill the
  days and nights
With music, and the world
  is listening to its melodies.
Mad with joy, Life and Death
  dance to the rhythm of this music.
The hills and the sea and the earth dance:
The world of man danceth in
  laughter and tears.
Why put on the robe of the
  monk, and live aloof from
  the world in lonely pride?
Behold! my heart danceth
  in the delight of a hundred
  arts
and the Creator is well pleased.

From **London Visions** *by* Laurence Binyon

THE LITTLE DANCERS

Lonely, save for a few faint stars, the sky
Dreams; and lonely, below, the little street
Into its gloom retires, secluded and shy
Scarcely the dumb roar enters this soft retreat;
And all is dark, save where come flooding rays
From a tavern window: there, to the brisk measure
Of an organ that down in an alley merrily plays,
Two children, all alone and no one by,
Holding their tattered frocks, through an airy maze
Of motion lightly threaded with nimble feet
Dance sedately: face to face they gaze,
Their eyes shining, grave with a perfect pleasure.

THE SCULPTOR

'No soul, no sculpture'

From **The Agony and the Ecstasy** *by* Irving Stone

Michelangelo speaking with Galli:

'You're like an engineer,' said Galli when he saw it, his expression rapt as he traced Michelangelo's design.

'That's what I told Bertoldo, a sculptor had to be'.

'In the days of the emperors you would have been designing colosseums, baths and reservoirs. Instead you've created a soul.'

Michelangelo's eyes glowed yellow at the compliment.

'No soul, no sculpture.'

'Many of my ancient pieces were found broken in several places, yet when we put them together their spirit persisted.'

'That was the sculptor still alive in the marble.'

'If there is one thing I know for sure it's that, when I hold a hammer and chisel in my hands and start that "Go", I need my full assurance that I can do no wrong. I need my complete self-respect. Once let me know that I can be content with inferior work . . .' There was agony in his voice, a pleading with Sangallo to affirm this concept. '. . . And as an artist, I'm through.'

From **Consequently I Rejoice** *by* Elizabeth Jennings

MICHELANGELO'S FIRST PIETÀ

Carve a compassion. Older than you are
He lies upon your lap. What can you do
But hold him with a trust you also fear?
  Thus Michelangelo.

Saw what a girl may do for gods. O we
Have mercy on this man a woman holds,
God in the grip of our humanity.
  All this the sculptor moulds.

But more. It is a prayer that he is saying
Wordless, except that written on her breast
He writes his name. This girl he is displaying
  Has also brought him rest.

From **Observations** *by* Henry Moore *in* **Eight European Artists**

Some Notes on Space and Form in Sculpture
One distorts the forms in order to create space. . . . If space is a willed, a wished-for element in the sculpture, then some distortion of the form—to ally itself to the space—is necessary.

At one time the holes in my sculpture were made for their own sakes. Because I was trying to become conscious of spaces in the sculpture, I made the hole have a shape in its own right, the solid body was encroached upon, eaten into, and sometimes the form was only the shell holding the hole. Recently I have attempted to make the forms and the spaces (not holes) inseparable, neither being more important than the other. In the last bronze Reclining Figure I think I have in some measure succeeded in this aim. What I mean is perhaps most obvious if this figure is looked at lengthwise from the head end through to the foot end, and the arms, body, legs, elbows etc. are seen as forms in recession inhabiting a tunnel. Seen in plan the figure has 'pools' of space.

Sculptors' Drawings
There is a general idea that sculptors' drawings should be diagramatic studies, without any sense of a background behind the object or of any atmosphere around it. That is, the object is stuck on the

flat surface of the paper with no attempt to set it in space—and often not even to connect it with the ground, with gravity.

And yet the sculptor is as much concerned with space as the painter. He must make the object he draws capable of having a far side to it, that is, make it an object in space, not an object in relief (only half an object stuck on the paper, and stopping at its edges). It is necessary to give it the possibility of an existence beyond the surface of the paper. Any wash, smudge, shading, anything breaking the tyranny of the flat plane of the paper, opens up a suggestion, a possibility of SPACE.

From **It Won't Last For Ever But It's Not Done Yet** *by* Patrick Mace

THE SCULPTOR

I saw God in this. In stone.
My chisel trapped an angel in a block of stone
And day by day I hammered out a dream
Till my stone angel took my breath and lived—
Spirituality in stone—your epitaph says,
There, in the corner, where her ruin is;
Time has reversed my chisel's trace,
Time, and man's malice and the wear in things.
My splintered angel now lacks limbs and face
And begs your charity for what she was.
Do not stay by her long,
Do not waste effort tracing my dead passion
But find one among yourselves with hands enough
To hammer a vision for your own age's fashion.
Look, there waits your angel in the stone.

From **The English Poems of George Herbert**

THE CHURCH FLOOR

Mark you the floore? that square and speckled stone,
  Which looks so firm and strong,
    Is *Patience*.

And th'other black and grave, wherewith each one
  Is checker'd all along
    Humilitie:

The gentle rising, which on either hand
  Leads to the Quire above,
    Is *Confidence*:

But the sweet Cement, which in one sure band
  Ties the whole frame, is *Love*
    And Charitie.

  Hither sometimes Sinne steals, and stains
  The Marble's neat and curious veins:
But all is cleansed when the Marble weeps.
  Sometimes Death, puffing at the doore,
  Blows all the dust about the floore:
But while he thinks to spoil the room, he sweeps.
  Blest be the Architect, whose art
  Could build so strong in a weak heart!

From **Selected Poems** *by* Mervyn Peake

EL GRECO

They spire terrific bodies into heaven,
Tall saints enswathed in a tempestuous flare
Of frozen draperies that twist through air,
Of dye incredible, from rapture thieven,
And heads set steeply skyward brittle carven
Pale upon coiling cloud in regions rare.
Their beauty, ice-like, shrills, and everywhere
A metal music sounds, cold spirit grieven.

So drives the acid nail of coloured pain
Into our vulnerable wood earth-rooted,
And sends the red sap racing through the trees
Where slugged it lay—now spun with visions looted
From whining skies, and sharp Gethsemanes
Of hollow light and all the wounds of Spain.

By G. K. Chesterton

STONEMASONS

We have graven the mountain of God with hands,
As our hands were graven of God, they say,
Where the seraphs burn in the sun like brands
And the devils carry the rains away:
Making a thrift of the throats of hell,
Our gargoyles gather the roaring rain,
Whose yawn is more than a frozen yell
And their very vomiting not in vain. . . .

We have graven the forest of heaven with hands,
Being great with a mirth too gross for pride,
In the stone that battered him Stephen stands
And Peter himself is petrified:
Such hands as have grubbed in the glebe for bread
Have bidden the blank rock blossom and thrive,
Such hands as have stricken a live man dead
Have struck, and stricken the dead alive. . . .

Fold your hands before heaven in praying.
Lift up your hands into heaven, and cry;
But look where our dizziest spires are saying
What the hands of man did up in the sky:
Drenched before you have heard the thunder;
White before you have felt the snow;
For the giants lift up their heads to wonder
How high the hands of a man could go.

From **Selected Poems** *by* D. H. Lawrence

WHATEVER MAN MAKES

Whatever man makes and makes it live
lives because of the life put into it.
A yard of India muslin is alive with Hindu life.
And a Navajo woman weaving her rug in the pattern of
her dream
must run the pattern out in a little break at the end
so that her soul can come out, back to her.

But in the odd pattern, like snake-marks on the sand
it leaves its trail.

From **Markings** *by* Dag Hammarskjöld

Without our being aware of it, our fingers are so guided that a pattern is created when the thread gets caught in the web.

From **Out of the Whirlwind: A Play for Westminster Abbey** *by* Christopher Hassall

Chorus: Surely they builded well who shaped the barren rock
And wrought a spiritual thing.
Rough hands grew gnarled and old the chisel rusty.
Creatures of decay, craftsmen in marble that wears away,
Their human summers withered into winter;
But slowly, slowly out of the dust whereto their toil gave meaning,
Slowly there arose like the sun in daybreak splendour,
Strengthening, not failing with the continual years,
An image in the minds of their children's children,
A Temple of the heart, a dwelling for the Holy Ghost.
Surely they builded well who shaped the barren rock
And wrought a spiritual thing, a song of praise
For all men who come hither to behold and sing.

By Anne Born, *quoted in* **The Countryman**

DRY STONE WALLS

These lines on the undulated earth
and under the variety of skies
run always towards perfection
Hillmen know it is wise
to build with what's near them,

to roll stone down from above,
not drag foreign elements upward.
Stone's matured longer than wood
and can be trusted to stay hard.
Look. See in it all that is good

in substance, texture and shade
for land's framing, hand's skill,
eye's grace and mind's freedom.
The dyker making his wall will
select the fitting stones, know them

with quick affinity, so they stay
accepting, filtering wind, rain,
all weather, through their spaces,
because they're allowed this gain
to poise free in air. Compare the faces

of mortared houses, blocks, stones
expressionless in flatness.
Then look at these airy lines
of relationship whose balance
marks strength in long durable lines.

THE MUSICIAN

'Music expresses that which cannot be put into words and that which cannot remain silent'

From **The Complete Poems** *by* Walter de la Mare

MUSIC

When music sounds, gone is the earth I know,
And all her lovely things even lovelier grow;
Her flowers in vision flame, her forest trees
Lift burdened branches, stilled with ecstasies.

When music sounds, out of the water rise
Naiads whose beauty dims my waking eyes,
Rapt in strange dreams burns each enchanted face,
With solemn echoing stirs their dwelling place.

When music sounds, all that I was I am
Ere to this haunt of brooding dust I came;
While from Time's woods break into distant song
The swift-winged hours, as I hasten along.

From **A Tent in Which to Pass a Summer's Night**
by Belle Valerie Gaunt and George Trevelyan

TUNING THE INSTRUMENT HERE AT THE DOOR

Since I am coming to that Holy roome
Where, with thy Quire of Saints, for evermore
I shall be made thy music; as I come
I tune the instrument here at the door,
And what I must doe then, thinke here before.

These words by John Donne direct our attention to the very heart of the purpose of our life on this earth. They stir our imagination and provoke what Wordsworth calls 'obstinate questionings'. How are we to set about this tuning of our instrument, here in the ante-room of earth-life, before joining the great orchestra in the next dimension? Donne's powerful poetic imagery sets fire to our imagination. He is suggestive, not dogmatic, and we are left free to speculate and to undertake our own 'adventures in ideas'. Whatever our beliefs or prejudices about survival after physical death may be, we shall probably be familiar with the concept of many different levels of consciousness; and it is in this direction that we may find an interpretation of Donne's poem.

A wise teacher has said that even a little knowledge and understanding of the next sphere (for which we are all bound, whether we like it or not) will be of great value to us. If the next world is indeed largely a thought world; Donne's words are fraught with a sense of urgency that underlines the spiritual law of cause and effect: as we think now, so shall we *be* when we discard the body. The metaphor of music, implying a vast orchestra in which we all participate, draws our attention to the possibility of unity in diversity, and to the underlying quality of harmony. Any orchestra would be the poorer if all the instruments were playing the same line of music: the secret lies in perfect blending. Implicit in Donne's image is the suggestion that each one of us will contribute a degree of harmony, or lack of it, according to the quality of thought and character built up through a possible succession of lives. 'As a man thinketh in his heart, so is he.'

From **Selected Poems (Tares)** *by* R. S. Thomas

THE MUSICIAN

A memory of Kreisler once:
At some recital in this same city,
The seats all taken, I found myself pushed
On to the stage with a few others,

So near that I could see the toil
Of his face muscles, a pulse like a moth
Fluttering under the fine skin
And the indelible veins of his smooth brow.

I could see, too, the twitching of the fingers,
Caught temporarily in art's neurosis,
As we sat there or warmly applauded
This player who so beautifully suffered
For each of us upon his instrument.
So it must have been on Calvary
In the fiercer light of the thorns' halo:
The men standing by and that one figure,
The hands bleeding, the mind bruised but calm,
Making such music as lives still.
And no one daring to interrupt
Because it was himself that he played
And closer than all of them the God listened.

From Intimations of Christianity *by* Simone Weil

The cry of the Christ and the silence of the Father together make the supreme harmony, that harmony of which all music is but an intimation, that to which our harmonies, those at once the most heartbreaking and the most sweet, bear an infinitely far away and dim resemblance. The whole universe including our own existences as tiny fragments of it, is only the vibration of that harmony.

From Revelation: Letters Written From the Other Side of Death

Remember happiness is not contentment, it is knowing that you are living up to the fullest that God means you to live. It means getting all that God is giving you instead of shelling out a good deal of it by not being ready to receive it. He is giving you so much and your hearts should be singing for all the love that is being poured into your whole being, and when you awaken from the dream of sorrow and see the radiance that surrounds you, you will be amazed at the glory of it all and your own blindness in not knowing it was there.

Be careful not to stop the gifts of God from reaching you by not being ready to receive them: that is the sin against the Holy Ghost for which there can be no forgiveness, because if you stop the power and the love and the life that are meant to be yours from reaching you there can be no hope for you excepting the hammerings of sorrow and disaster which may ultimately make you open up your hearts and minds to receive the great gifts which have been at your very door.

Be careful not to delay, because the longer you keep out the gifts of the spirit from you the thicker grows the veil between you and light, till the glimmer becomes so faint that you can scarcely see it at all, even when you want to.

There is, however, no hopelessness really.

We may have arrived at the last string on the lyre but it will not break for us if we go on trying to play. If we do this, gradually the mist will clear away and we shall see by the full light that the strings to mend the lyre are close at hand, and we shall soon be ready to take our place in God's perfect orchestra which is the company of all the faithful whether here on earth or in the great beyond, which is beyond even our ken here.

Have your lyres ready to play, your minds attuned to God and do not be disconsolate if your part in the orchestra seems too hard for you to play. From the smallest part to the biggest they are all too difficult for the performers, because otherwise they would never learn to be better musicians. It is so easy to watch other people playing and to think one would be able to play their part so much easier than one's own. One's own part is the only part that one could play, so let us be contented to go on making the very best melody out of it that one can. Be sure to be humble about it and never let yourself think that you are a good musician if you seem to be playing your part correctly and not crashing down on the wrong notes, because it will only mean that you have been endowed with a ear for music and have been well taught. Besides always know that you could be doing it better than you are; you could be getting more out of it.

There is no end to the message you can give out from a perfectly played piece of music.

Anonymous

Music leads us to the edge of the infinite and lets us for a moment look therein with wonder.

From **Siegfried's Journey** *by* Siegfried Sassoon

1917. My next January entry commemorates a concert in Liverpool at which I heard Elgar's Violin Concerto for the first time, an emotional experience which my afterthoughts impelled me to report in terms that had, it now seems, little relation to the music.

In all the noblest passages of this glorious work I shut my eyes, seeing on the darkness a shape always the same—the suffering mortal figure on a cross. And around it a host of shadowy forms with upraised arms—the souls of men, agonized and aspiring, hungry for what they seek as God in vastness and confoundment. This is followed by a poem which I now find just worth rescuing from the page where it has remained hidden since I scribbled it in a fine—and perhaps foolish—frenzy.

I have seen Christ when music wove
Majestic vision. Storms of prayer
Deep-voiced within me marched and strove.
The sorrows of the world were there.

A god for beauty shamed and wronged,
A sign where faith and ruin meet
In glooms of vanquished glory thronged
By Spirits blinded with defeat,
His head for ever bowed in pain,
I feel his presence plead above
The violin that speaks in vain
The crowned humility of love.

O music undeterred by death
And darkness closing on your flame,
Christ whispers in your dying breath
And haunts you with his tragic name.

By Ludwig van Beethoven

MUSIC IN THE MIND

You will ask where I find my ideas: I hardly know. They come uninvited, directly or indirectly. I can almost grasp them with my hands in the open air, in the woods while walking, in the stillness of the night, early in the morning, called up by the moods which the poet translates into words, I into musical tones. They ring and roar and swirl about me until I write them down in notes.

From **St Francis of Assisi** *by* Elizabeth Goudge

But all that day he went on thinking of the beauty of music, until with the coming of night his thoughts were filled with the thought of the beauty of God. When night was in the midst of her course, and the little town lay still, Francis was alone and awake in the darkness. There was complete silence, very heavenly, and then gently and gradually entering into the silence, music. Someone was playing the viol under his window. The musician touched his instrument with an unearthly skill, and the music sounded now here, now there, as though the player were passing gently back and forth.

Yet there was no sound of footsteps, only that heavenly music, such music as Francis had not heard since the angel had played to him on Alvernia. He forgot his pain for in the place to which the music lifted him there was no suffering.

By Yehudi Menuhin

Music is the mirror of the heart and the mind of the composer and the player.

From **Prayers of Grief and Glory** *by* Richard Harries

CECILIA

Music seems to say something but we can never put into words just what it is saying. It seems to take us beyond words. The composer Mahler once wrote, 'As long as my experience can be summed up in words, I write no music about it, my need to express myself musically . . . begins at the door which leads into the "other world"—the world in which things are no longer separated by space and time.' And a contemporary Christian, Ulrich Simon, has stated the same thought in these words, 'For me the D minor quartet and the C minor quintet of Mozart evoke in every bar the truth about God, but I do not know how to express the truth. Perhaps it is a *musical* truth, for what do words like "tragic" and "searing" mean, even if I related them to my chosen bars, themes and developments? Rather these empty words are fulfilled by the music. We owe everything to Mozart because he has revealed the priority of music in theology.'

Music, then, seems to lead us into another world, to make us aware of the spiritual dimension, in a way that words so often fail to do.

From **The Memorial Service for Hugh Allen in Westminster Abbey**

Almighty and Everlasting God, of whom alone cometh the voice of melody, pour thy grace, we humbly pray thee, on all musicians: that to thee first they may ever tender each gift of music and the power of song.

From **Conversations With Kafka** *by* Gustav Janouch

Everything that lives is in flux. Everything that lives emits sound. But we only perceive a part of it. We do not hear the circulation of the blood, the growth and decay of our bodily tissue, the sound of our chemical processes. But our delicate organic cells, the fibres of brain and nerves and skin are impregnated with these inaudible sounds. They vibrate in response to their environment. This is the foundation of the power of music. We can set free these profound emotional vibrations. In order to do so, we employ musical instruments, in which the decisive factor is their own inner sound potential. That is to say: what is decisive is not the strength of the sound, or its tonal colour, but its hidden character, the intensity with which its musical power affects the nerves. This is the fundamental problem of every musical instrument and every instrument maker. He must try and endow his instrument with the highest possible degree of tonal intensity. That is to say: he must construct instruments which elevate into human consciousness vibrations which are otherwise inaudible and unperceived. The instrument maker's problem is therefore that of bringing silence to life. He must uncover the hidden sound of silence.

THE POET

Poetry 'compels us to feel that which we perceive, and to imagine that which we know'

From **Towards Democracy** *by* Edward Carpenter

How shall I say what I have to say? How shall I speak the word which sums up all words that are spoken? How shall I speak that for which the moon and the stars and running waters and the universe itself subsist, to speak it?—which if it could be uttered in a word there would be no need of all these things.

From **A Defence of Poetry** *by* P. B. Shelley

Poetry turns all things to loveliness; it exalts the beauty of that which is most beautiful, and it adds beauty to that which is most deformed; it marries exultation and horror, grief and pleasure, eternity and change; it subdues to union, under its light yoke, all irreconcilable things. It transmutes all that it touches, and every form moving within the radiance of its presence is changed by wondrous sympathy to an incarnation of the spirit which it breathes: its secret alchemy turns to potable gold the poisonous waters which flow from death through life; it strips the veil of familiarity from the world, and lays bare the naked and sleeping beauty, which is the spirit of its forms. . . . It purges from our inward sight the film of familiarity which obscures from us the wonder of our being. It compels us to feel that which we perceive, and to imagine that which we know.

Anonymous

Poetry, by its intense use of language, is able to express the furthest reaches of the human spirit.

From **The Complete Poems** *by* Walter de la Mare

THE SCRIBE

What lovely things
  Thy hand hath made:
The smooth-plumed bird
  In its emerald shade,
The seed of the grass,
  The speck of stone
Which the wayfaring ant
  Stirs—and hastes on!

Though I should sit
  By some tarn in thy hills,
Using its ink
  As the spirit wills
To write of Earth's wonders,
  Its live, willed things,
Flit would the ages
  On soundless wings
Ere unto Z
  My pen drew nigh;
Leviathan told
  And the honey-fly:
And still would remain
  My wit to try—
My worn reeds broken,
  The dark tarn dry,
All words forgotten—
  Thou, Lord, and I.

From **The Moment of Truth** *by* Ladislaus Boros

R. M. Rilke in his Notebook of Malte Laurids Brigge described poetic creation as the conservation and fitting together of a whole life's scattered experiences of meaning and lucidity.

Poetry is not, as so many people think a question of feelings but of experiences. For the sake of a single line one needs to see many Cities, men and things, to know animals, to feel how birds fly, to have learnt the gesture with which flowers open in the morning. One must be able to think back to paths in unknown regions, to unexpected meetings and partings one had seen coming long before they actually occurred, to childhood days still shrouded in mist, to parents one could not help hurting when they brought one some joy or other and one did not understand—it was joy for someone else—to children's sicknesses that begin so strangely with such deep and trying metamorphoses, to days in quiet, modest rooms, and mornings by the sea, to the sea itself, to seas, to nights on board ship rushing past high in the sky, flying with all the stars. And even to think back to all that is still not enough. One needs to have memories of many nights of love, none of them like any of its fellows, of the cries of women in labour, and then of how light and white they are as they lie sleeping and shrinking back into shape after they have given birth. Then one must have stood by as men died, kept watch by the dead in a room with the window wide open and the short, sharp rustling noises. And it is not enough merely to have memories. One must be able to forget them if they are many, and have the great patience to wait until they come again, for the memories themselves are not yet the thing. Only when they become blood, sight and gesture in us, nameless and indistinguishable from ourself, only then may it happen that in a very special hour the first word of a line arises among them and comes forth.

From **Gitanjali** *by* Rabindranath Tagore

LXV

What divine drink wouldst thou have, my God, from this overflowing cup of my life?

My poet, is it thy delight to see thy creation through my eyes and to stand at the portals of my ears silently to listen to thine own eternal harmony?

Thy world is weaving words in my mind and thy joy is adding music to them. Thou givest thyself to me in love and then feelest thine own entire sweetness in me.

From **Later Poems** *by* Rainer Maria Rilke

O, tell us poet, what you do?—I praise
But those dark, deadly, devastating ways,
   how do you bear them, suffer them? I praise.
And then the Nameless, beyond guess or gaze,
   how can you call it, conjure it? I praise.
And whence your right, in every kind of maze,
   in every mask, to remain true? I praise.
And that the mildest and the wildest ways
   know you like star and storm?—Because I praise.

From **Yes To God** *by* Alan Ecclestone

Browning's poetry deals with what is essentially the business of prayer, the responsive Yes that a man must endeavour to make in those moments when the engagement is offered to him, when to be truly himself he must speak the truth, in love, when he is presented with the opportunity and the responsibility of framing his reply 'in spirit and in truth'. Browning knew that the eternal Word waited to be embodied in human speech. In such moments all the divine events from the Nativity to the Passion are in our human key re-enacted. The Word may be given no room may be misunderstood, treated with contempt, entirely rejected, but it is certain that, because of His love, it will not cease to be uttered. It is in this sense that the language of poetry is the serious speech to which all prayer aspires. The poet knows only too well that he himself is failing again and again to speak as he should, now wrestling with unmanagable perceptions, now giving way to the deceptions of easy speech, now intruding a false self-consciousness into the area where openness should prevail. The poet can just as easily get in the way of the movement of the Word as anyone else. He may be all that Shelley said so magnificently about the poet and still betray his calling. Nevertheless he shares in the forgiveness extended to us all. It is his job to enable words to become bearers of the Word, to permit the Word to take our flesh and dwell among us, to speak the words that hallow all that God has given and man has received, to translate them all into Yes to God.

From **Tentative Definitions of Poetry** *by* Carl Sandburg

Poetry is the achievement of the synthesis of hyacinths and biscuits. . . Poetry is the journal of a sea animal living on land, wanting to fly the air. . .

Poetry is a theorem of a yellow-silk handkerchief knotted with riddles, sealed in a balloon tied to the tail of a kite flying in a white wind against a blue sky in spring. . . Poetry is the opening and closing of a door, leaving those who look through to guess about what is seen during a moment.

From **One Word of Truth,** Nobel prize speech 1970 *by* Alexander Solzhenitsyn

Woe betide that nation whose literature is interrupted by the interference of force. This is not simply a violation of the 'freedom of the press': it is the locking-up of the national heart, the carving-up of the national memory. Such a nation does not remember itself, it is deprived of its spiritual unity, and although its population supposedly have a common language, fellow-countrymen suddenly stop understanding each other. Mute generations live out their lives and die without telling their story either to their own or a future generation. If such geniuses as Akhmatova or Zamyatin are walled up alive for the duration of their lives, if they are condemned to create in silence until the grave, without hearing any response to what they have written, then this is not just their own personal misfortune but the deep tragedy of a whole nation—and, too, a threat to the whole nation. And in certain cases it is a danger for the whole of mankind, too: when the whole of history ceases to be understood because of that silence.

From **Jesus, Son of Man** *by* Kahlil Gibran

RUMANOUS: A GREEK POET

He was a poet. He saw for our eyes and heard for our ears, and our silent words were upon His lips; and His fingers touched what we could not feel.

Out of His heart there flew countless singing birds to the north and to the south, and the little flowers on the hill-sides stayed His steps toward the heavens.

Oftentimes I have seen Him bending down to touch the blades of grass. And in my heart I have heard Him say: 'Little green things, you shall be with me in my kingdom even as the oaks of Besan, and the Cedars of Lebanon.'

He loved all things of loveliness, the shy faces of Children, and the myrrh and frankincense from the south.

He loved a pomegranate or a cup of wine given Him in kindness: it mattered not whether it was offered by a stranger in the inn or by a rich host.

And he loved the almond blossoms. I have seen Him gathering them into His hands and covering His face with the petals, as though He would embrace with His love all the trees in the world.

He knew the sea and the heavens; and He spoke of pearls which have light that is not of this light, and of stars that are beyond our night. He knew the mountains as eagles knew them, and the valleys as they are known by the brooks and the streams. And there was a desert in His silence and a garden in His speech.

Aye He was a poet whose heart dwelt in a bower beyond the heights and His songs though sung for our ears, were sung for other ears also, and to men in another land where life is for ever young and time is always dawn.

Once I too deemed myself a poet, but when I stood before Him in Bethany. I knew what it is to hold an instrument with but a single string before one who commands all instruments. For in His voice there was the laughter of thunder and the tears of rain, and the joyous dancing of trees in the wind. And since I have known that my lyre has but one string and that my voice weaves neither the memories of yesterday nor the hopes of tomorrow, I have put aside my lyre and I shall keep silence. But always at twilight I shall hearken to the Poet who is the sovereign of all poets.

From **Poems** *by* Dorothea Eastwood

PRAYER FOR A POET

God, of your pity give him greater strength
To bear these wonders loaded on his soul;
God, of your pity think of what you ask—
Jack Poet to be spokesman for the Whole.

This tongue of fire you have equipped him with
Burns in a mouth that sucked a human breast,
These curbless spring tides plunging in the blood
Thunder through limbs that, childish, weep for rest.

How can he gaze at you, with cosmic gaze
That looks between the stars, sleepless all night?
How can he voice it? This voice of the worlds
Which speaks through a dove flying in the morning light.

Yet look he must, although the fierce stars blind,
And speak he must, although the gold-winged bird
Turn vulture on his heart, although you, God,
Decree his singing shall be never heard:

For he is that stringed lute on which you play
Music his love's capacity can sound,
And he, Musician, is your melody,
Singing of Heaven and man's mortal wound.

From **Conversations With Kafka** *by* Gustav Janouch

'Aggression is usually only a disguise which conceals one's weakness from oneself and from the world. Genuine and lasting strength consists in bearing things. Only weaklings react quickly and brutally. And in doing so, they sacrifice their manhood.'

Kafka opened the drawer of his desk and took out a magazine . . . which he placed in front of me.

He said to me: 'On the first page there are four poems. One is very touching. It's called *Pokora*—Humility.' I read:

I'll grow smaller and smaller
Till I'm the smallest thing on earth.
On an early morning, in a summer meadow
I'll stretch my hand to the smallest flower

And hide my face in it, whispering:
On you, little child, without shoes or clothes,
Heaven leans its hand
In a flashing drop of dew
So that its giant sky
Shan't break in pieces.

I said quietly: 'That is poetry.'

'Yes', answered Kafka, 'that is poetry—Truth clothed in the language of friendship and love. Everything, the prickliest thistle just as much as the most elegant palm tree supports the heavenly firmament above us, so that the giant sky, the giant sky of our world, shan't break in pieces.'

From **One Word of Truth** Nobel prize speech 1970 *by* Alexander Solzhenitsyn

In my opinion it is within the powers of world literature in these troubled times to help humanity to comprehend its own nature in spite of what is being instilled into people's minds by biased persons and parties. World literature can transmit the concentrated experience of one land to another in such a way that we stop seeing double and being dazzled, the different scales of values coincide, and each nation can learn the true history of other nations in an accurate, condensed form, grasping it fully with that sensation of pain that comes from living an experience oneself, and as a result of that knowledge be protected from eventual error. And we writers in so doing may perhaps develop our own world vision: we shall use the centre of our eye, like everybody else, to see what is near, and use the corners of our eye to begin absorbing what is happening in the rest of the world. And then we can compare and relate things on a world-wide scale.

And who, if not writers, can censure not only their own inadequate leaders (in some states this is the easiest bread of all to earn; anyone who is not too lazy is busy doing it) but also their own society, whether for its cowardly self-humiliation or for its smug weakness? Who but writers can reprove the thoughtless excesses of youth, and those young pirates with their threatening knives? We shall be asked, 'What can literature do in the face of the merciless onslaught of open violence?' But let us not forget that violence does not exist alone and cannot survive in isolation: it is inevitably bound up with the lie.

Between them there is the most intimate, most natural, fundamental link: violence can only be concealed by the lie, and the lie can be maintained only by violence. Anyone who has once proclaimed that violence is his method is inevitably forced to choose the lie as his guiding principle. At its birth violence acts openly, is even proud of itself. But it has scarcely established itself when it feels the air around it becoming more rarefied, and it cannot continue to exist without masking itself with the lie and wrapping itself up in its honeyed rhetoric. Violence does not always necessarily take you physically by the throat and strangle you: more often it merely demands of its subjects that they declare allegiance to the lie, become accomplices in the lie.

And the simple step of a simple, courageous man is not to take part in the lie, not to support deceit. Let the lie come into the world, even dominate the world, but not through me. Moreover, writers and artists can do something more: they can vanquish the lie. Wherever else it fails. Art always has won its fight against lies, and it will always win. Its victory will be obvious, irrevocably obvious to all men. The lie can withstand a great deal in this world but it cannot withstand Art.

Once the lie has been dispersed, the nakedness of violence will be revealed in all its repulsiveness, and then violence, become decrepit, will come crashing down.

That is why I think, my friends, that we are capable of helping the world in its agonised testing hour. We must not seek excuses on the grounds that we lack weapons, we must not give ourselves over to a carefree life, we must go out into battle.

From **Collected Poems of Kathleen Raine**

THE SPHERE

This poem gathers together all our longings into one single glorious whole.

O the happy ending, the happy ending
That the fugue promised, that love believed in,
That perfect star, that bright transfiguration,

Where has it vanished, now that the music is over,
The certainty of being, the heart in flower,
Ourselves, perfect at last, affirmed as what we are?

The world, the changing world stands still while lovers kiss,
And then moves on—what was our fugitive bliss,
The dancer's ecstasy, the vision, and the rose?

There is no end, no ending—steps of a dance, petals of flowers,
Phrases of music, rays of the sun, the hours
Succeed each other, and the perfect sphere
Turns in our hearts the past and future, near and far,
Our single soul, atom, and universe.

Part IV

PRAYING

DREAMING

DYING

PRAYING

'Prayer is a means by which the power of the love of God is released into the world'

Romans 8:24–9, The Common Bible

Now hope that is seen is not hope. For who hopes for what he sees? But if we hope for what we do not see, we wait for it with patience. Likewise the Spirit helps us in our weakness; for we do not know how to pray as we ought, but the Spirit himself intercedes for us with sighs too deep for words. And he who searches the hearts of men knows what is the mind of the Spirit, because the Spirit intercedes for the saints according to the will of God.

We know that in everything God works for good with those who love him, who are called according to his purpose.

From **Rule for a New Brother** *by* H. van der Looy

Remember that your prayer is more powerful than anything you can achieve by your actions.

From an article by George Appleton in **The Daily Telegraph**

HOPELESS SITUATIONS?

The present situation is making us aware of how much we depend on one another. For years I have valued a prayer by a great American scholar and theologian, Reinhold Niebuhr, perhaps more in theory and principle than in immediate relevance and practical urgency. It runs:

O God, who has bound us together in this bundle of life, give us grace to understand how our lives depend upon the courage, the industry, the honesty and the integrity of our fellow-men, that we may be mindful of their needs, grateful for their faithfulness, and faithful in our responsibilities to them.

In praying this prayer in our chronic emergency, I find questions arising in my mind of how the prayer of a few individuals can have any effect on such a desperate and widespread situation. That thought reveals a lack of faith in God, the Eternal Spirit who created us all, with a capacity to know Him, who asks us to co-operate with Him in building a world of human relationships in accordance with his wise, good and loving will.

Prayer in desperate situations keeps these situations tied to God. It prevents God being pushed out of them. Every praying person affords a link with Him through which the energy of love may be piped to the points where it is most needed. It makes us aware that we are all bound together in our common life, aware both of others and of God. There is live contact at both ends.

To affect the situation an adequate number of praying people may be required. I sometimes think of our common consciousness as being like a great web, spreading out to cover the whole of humanity, with each of us a knot in the web, able to send out impulses to the nearby knots and ultimately into the whole net of human relationships.

If I really believe in God, I shall also believe that He will use the link that I make with Him and the human situation, realising that it may take quite a time to influence a chronic situation. I learn also from experience that quiet, persistent prayer can reveal the hidden possibilities in seemingly hopeless situations, suggest new initiatives and engender undefeatable hope.

Prayer *by* Peter Roberts

God of all nations, we pray thee for all the people of thy earth; for those who are consumed in mutual hatreds and bitterness; for those who make war upon their neighbours; for those who tyrannously oppress; for those who groan under cruelty and subjection. We beseech thee to teach mankind to live together in peace, no man exploiting the weak, no man hating the strong, each race working out its own destiny, unfettered, self-respecting, fearless.

Teach us to be worthy of freedom, free from social wrong, free from individual oppression and contempt, pure of heart and hand, despising none, defrauding none, giving to all men—in all dealings of life—the honour we owe to those who are thy children, whatever their colour, their race or their caste.

From an article by Henry Thomas Hamblin *in* **The Science of Thought Review**

DRAWING HEAVEN DOWN TO EARTH

It has been said that the safety of a nation depends upon the number of its contemplatives.

. . . While they contemplate the Supernal worlds, they become filled with Heavenly peace, after which Divine Light and Love flow through them to earth.

Consequently the more genuine contemplatives there are the more love and peace will there be manifested on the earth.

There is a pool of tranquility within each one of us, a centre of silence and peace. There the whole being may be renewed. There the strength of the Father may be felt. To sit beside this pool at least once each day is to replenish and rejuvenate our being.

Without this period of silence and contemplation our whole life starts to disintegrate into chaos, frustration and despair. We have then cut ourselves off from our source and from our purpose.

The more often we can find a moment or two to sit beside our pool of stillness, the greater will be our strength, for then our strength is the strength of the Father as he works His Will through us and we will dwell in the house of the Lord for ever.

From **The Practice of Prayer** *by* George Appleton

O Spirit of God, set at rest the crowded, hurrying anxious thoughts within our minds and hearts. Let the peace and quiet of thy presence take possession of us. Help us to rest, to relax, to become open and receptive to Thee. Thou dost know our inmost spirits, the hidden unconscious life within us, the forgotten memories of hurts and fears, the frustrated desires, the unresolved tensions and dilemmas. Cleanse and sweeten the springs of our being, that freedom, life and love may flow into both our conscious and hidden life. Lord, we lie open before Thee, waiting for Thy peace, thy healing and thy word.

By Père Grou (1731–1803), quoted in **The Practice of Prayer** *by* George Appleton

Teach us O God that silent language which says all things. Teach our souls to remain silent in thy presence that we may adore Thee in the deeps of our being and await all things from Thee, whilst asking of Thee nothing but the accomplishment of thy will. Teach us to remain quiet under thine action and produce in our souls that deep and simple prayer which says nothing and expresses everything, which specifies nothing and expresses everything.

From **A Nip in the Air** *by* John Betjeman

GREEK ORTHODOX

. . . The domed interior swallows up the day.
Here, where to light a candle is to pray,
The candle flame shows up the almond eyes
Of local saints who view with no surprise
Their martyrdoms depicted upon walls
On which the filtered daylight faintly falls.
The flame shows up the cracked paint—sea-green blue
And red and gold, with grained wood showing through—
Of much kissed ikons, dating from, perhaps,
The fourteenth century . . .
Thus vigorously does the old tree grow,
By persecution pruned, watered with blood,

Its living roots deep in pre-Christian mud.
It needs no bureaucratical protection.
It is its own perpetual resurrection . . .

From Sadhana: A Way to God *by* Anthony de Mello

You may be one of those persons whom the Lord calls, in a very special way, to exercise the ministry of intercession and to transform the world and the hearts of men by the power of their prayers. '*Nothing is so powerful on earth as purity and prayer*', says Father Teilhard. If you have received this call from God then intercession will be your most common form of prayer. Even if you have not received the call to exercise the ministry of intercession in a special way, you will frequently feel impelled by God to intercede on various occasions. There are many ways of practising this form of prayer. Here is one:

Spend some time in becoming aware of the presence of Jesus and in getting in touch with him . . .

Imagine that Jesus floods you with his life and light and power . . . See the whole of your being, in imagination, lit up by this light that comes from him.

Now conjure up in imagination, one by one, the persons you wish to pray for. Lay your hands on each person, communicating to him all the life and power that you have just received from Christ. . . . Take your time over each individual . . . Call down Christ's love on him wordlessly . . . See him light up with Christ's life and love . . . See him transformed.

It is extremely important that you become aware of Jesus and get in touch with him at the beginning of your intercessory prayer. Otherwise your intercession is in danger of becoming not prayer, but a mere exercise of remembering people. The danger is that your attention will be focussed only on the people you are praying for and not on God.

After you have prayed for some people in the form suggested in the exercise it is helpful to rest awhile again in Christ's presence, drinking in his power, his Spirit, and then continue your intercession, laying hands on yet another person.

From **The Foolishness of God** *by* J. Austin Baker

Once we have grasped clearly what we are doing when we pray for others, we shall see that the most important requirement by far is inner calmness and tranquility. We are not engaged in creating or producing anything, but in becoming aware of what is already the fact, namely that God is immediately and intimately present both to ourselves and to the ones for whom we are praying. Our task is to hold the awareness of this fact in the still centre of our being, to unite our love for them with God's love, in the quiet but total confidence that he will use our love to help bring about the good in them which we both desire. In technical terms, therefore, intercession is a form of that kind of prayer known as 'contemplation', with the special feature that here we contemplate not God himself but God in his relationship of love towards those whom we also love; and on the basis of our partnership with him we entrust our love into his hands to be used in harness with his own for their benefit.

Teach us, O Father, to trust Thee with life and with death,
And (though this is harder by far)
With the life and death of those that are dearer to us than our life.

Teach us stillness and confident peace
In thy perfect will,
Deep calm of soul and content
In what Thou wilt do with these lives Thou hast given,

Teach us to wait and be still,
To rest in Thyself,
To hush the clamorous anxiety,
To lay in Thine arms all this wealth Thou hast given.

Thou lovest these souls that we love
With a love as far surpassing our own
As the glory of noon surpasses the gleam of a candle.
Therefore will we be still,
And trust in Thee.

[J. S. Hoyland]

From **Poems** *by* C. S. Lewis

From all my lame defeats and oh! much more
From all the victories that I seemed to score;
From cleverness shot forth on Thy behalf
At which, while angels weep, the audience laugh;
From all my proofs of Thy divinity;
Thou, who wouldst give no sign, deliver me. . . .
Lord of the narrow gate and the needle's eye,
Take from me all my trumpery lest I die.

Prayer for an Actor *by* Denys Blakelock

My Jesus, bless me in this my actor's life.
Whether I draw tears from an audience or make them laugh, off-stage let me be serious-minded, yet keep my sorrows behind the scenes. May I be undeceived by success and undismayed by failure. Make me generous towards the work of others and a good influence wherever I may go. Let me always return to the Sacraments, however often things go wrong.

On stage, off stage,
In life, in death,
Jesus have mercy
On my soul.

From **Christian Faith and Practice in the Experience of the Religious Society of Friends:** Section 460 *by* William Penn

Love silence, even in the mind . . . Much speaking, as much thinking, spends; and in many thoughts, as well as words, there is sin. True silence is the rest of the mind; and is to the spirit, what sleep is to the body, nourishment and refreshment.

From **Selected Poems 1946–68** *by* R. S. Thomas

KNEELING

Moments of great calm
Kneeling before an altar
of wood in a stone church
In summer, waiting for the God
To speak: the air a staircase
For silence; the sun's light
Ringing me, as though I acted
A great rôle. And the audience
Still; all that close throng
Of spirits waiting, as I,
For the message.
   Prompt me, God;
But not yet. When I speak,
Though it be you who speak
Through me, something is lost.
The meaning is in the waiting.

Isaiah 40:31, Authorized Version

But they that wait upon the Lord shall renew their strength; they shall mount up with wings as eagles; they shall run, and not be weary; and they shall walk, and not faint.

From **Truth: A Path and Not a Possession,** *Swarthmore Lecture 1977 by* Damaris Parker-Rhodes

TRANSCENDENTAL MEDITATION

Some brands of mysticism and meditation now currently claim to be seeking the development of human potential, while not believing in Christ, Buddha or Krishna. Where this quest is related to the search for wisdom and deeper truth about human values it is certainly a religious search, while desire for deep relaxation to relieve pressure, though not religious, may like other health and mental hygiene measures develop our maturity.

While that may be so, there is no doubt that any development of human potential has its possible misuse. Increased power must be increased power for either good or evil, for love and fellowship or for self-interest. Everything depends on what the goal or lack of goal may be. It is well known in all the great traditions that mystical powers can be used for either good or evil and for this reason it is necessary for Friends, and for all the great religions too, to understand how precious are their foundations in the divine and their own values. The emergence of mystical man can lead to further insecurity unless it is founded upon a gospel of love and a deep awareness of our incarnational place in the scheme of the universe. It is by this awareness that we are consciously able to unite with the saving work of the Cosmic Christ, so that the good works and the fellowship with one another for which we strive may find creative blessing.

. . . The Christian message is a deeply personal one. Where two or three are gathered together in Christ's name, he is there in the midst. . . .

This Presence makes perpetual demands on us and is the God of history, and at the same time is the source of our peace and the warmth of our inward fire. For us it is the personal presence of Christ, but it extends to a cosmic scale so that life begins to look like an intricate jigsaw puzzle—one is handed exactly the book one needs at that moment, or meets someone on a train who asks for just the precious knowledge one has lately gained. Again, a rebuke may come, or a piece of praise which checks or encourages in a way that is unaccountably helpful. This is indeed a network of love. Silence and love, rooted in the Gospel and the loving group, are the culture base in which the *seed of awareness* may grow. Beyond this we sometimes glimpse great reservoirs of peace and power not only equal to, but far more powerful than, the distractions and sufferings of the world.

Prayer *from* Malling Abbey

Be silent
still
aware
for there
in your own heart
The Spirit is at prayer
listen and learn
open and find
heart-wisdom
Christ.

A Seventeenth-Century Nun's Prayer

Lord, thou knowest, better than I know myself that I am growing older, and will soon be old.
Keep me from getting talkative, and particularly from the fatal habit of thinking I must say something on every occasion.
Release me from the craving to try and straighten out everybody's affairs.
Make me thoughtful but not moody, helpful but not bossy.
With my vast store of wisdom it seems a pity not to use it all!
But thou knowest, Lord, that I want a few friends at the end.
Keep my mind from the endless recital of details.
Give me wings to get to the point.
Seal my lips on many aches and pains; they are increasing and my love of rehearsing them is becoming sweeter as the years go by.
Teach me the glorious lesson that occasionally it is possible that I may be mistaken.
Keep me reasonably sweet.
I do not want to be a saint—some of them are hard to live with—but a sour old man or woman is one of the works of the devil.

From **The Practice of Prayer** *by* George Appleton

THE PRAYER OF LOVE

In Prayer for others, whether loved ones or people in trouble for whom we feel a concern . . . we act as a link between people in their need and God in his generosity of grace.

Such prayer is an expression of our compassion for people in their suffering, sins and needs, and our compassion grows deeper as we know more of their circumstances, whether as persons or communities. It denotes a growing understanding of the heartache of people, and at the same time a deepening conviction that it is love that saves heartache from becoming heartbreak. Prayer links the griefs and needs of people with the love and grace of God. We focus the love of God where the need is greatest. Our little human love calls to the infinitely greater love of God to come to the aid of those for whom we are concerned. We lift them up to His presence, hold them in His healing X-Ray, His radiant warmth, believing that whatever happens He is with them, all shall be well, nothing can snatch them out of His hand, however far they fall the everlasting arms are beneath.

. . . Our little impulses of love reach the over-arching love and are magnified by the divine energy which makes their transmission possible.

PRAYING WITH LOVE

O Thou source of all love,
let thy love go out to all created beings,
to those I love and to those who love me,
to the few I know and to the many I do not know,
to all of every race,
to all the living in this world
and to all the living dead in the next world:
May all be free from evil and harm
may all come to know thy love
and find the happiness
of loving Thee and their fellows
O let the small love of my heart
go out with thine all-embracing love
for the sake of him who first loved us
and taught us love even Jesus Christ our Lord.

Prayer *by* Gary Davies

Prayer is not just talking to oneself. Prayer is not even just talking to God. It is listening, seeing, understanding, doing. It is being spiritual farmers, harvesting a more enduring crop for the feeding of mankind. God has put man into a world where man must work and co-operate with the natural forces of life and growth around him. That has its spiritual counterpart too. In the realm of the Spirit man must also work and co-operate with the natural expressions of the Spirit that are around him. He must farm spiritually as well as materially. In prayer man is contributing in a way that he cannot yet measure for the health and wholeness of the collective mind, the group unconscious, the common psychic area in which we all swim. Fear and hatred grow at compound interest rates; so do love and peace. When we release the energy of fear into the world it is a real energy which affects and changes things. The same is true of love.

DREAMING

'We have heard the lute of Hope in sleep'

From **Prometheus Unbound** *by* P. B. Shelley

We have heard the lute of Hope in sleep;
We have known the voice of Love in dreams;
We have felt the wand of Power, and leap—
. . . As the billows leap in the morning beams!

From **The Inward Road and the Way Back**
by Dorothee Soelle

Sleep is a person's natural return into another condition, and in this sense we set out each night on the inward journey. We exchange our conscious condition for another, one in which we are helpless and unable to control life. We go back into an earlier stage of our conscious, adult existence.

Psalm 16:7, The Common Bible

I bless the Lord who gives me counsel;
in the night also my heart instructs me.

From **Theophanies** *by* Evelyn Underhill

FOR HILDA

. . . Strange poignant dreams the soul invade—
News from beyond our stubborn ramparts blown,
And here in perfume known.

Those ramparts they are builded tall;
But we a secret gate possess
That opens in the outer wall
What time its living latch we press;
A little emerald gate that sets us free
Within Eternity.

From **The Candle of Vision** *by* A. E.

THE AUTOBIOGRAPHY OF A MYSTIC

As I walked in the evening down the lanes scented by the honeysuckle my senses were expectant of some unveiling about to take place, I felt that beings were looking in upon me out of the true home of man. They seemed to be saying to each other of us, 'Soon they will awaken; soon they will come to us again,' and for a moment I almost seemed to mix with their eternity. The tinted air glowed before me with intelligible significance like a face, a voice. The visible world became like a tapestry blown and stirred by winds behind it. If it would but raise for an instant I knew I would be in Paradise. Every form on that tapestry appeared to be the work of gods. Every flower was a word, a thought. The grass was speech; the waters were speech; the winds were speech. They were the Army of the Voice marching on to conquest and dominion over the spirit; and I listened with my whole being.

. . . I knew these visitations for what they were and named them truly in my fantasy, for writing then in the first verses of mine which still seem to me to be poetry, I said of the earth that we and all things were her dreams:

She is rapt in dreams divine.
As her clouds of beauty pass
On our glowing hearts they shine,
Mirrored there as in a glass.

Earth, whose dreams are we and they,
With her deep heart's gladness fills
All our human lips can say
Or the dawn-fired singer trills.

From **Fairies and Fusiliers** *by* Robert Graves

DREAM BIRD

When a dream is born in you
  With a sudden clamorous pain,
When you know the dream is true
  And lovely, with no flaw nor stain.
O then, be careful, or with sudden clutch
You'll hurt the delicate thing you prize so much.

Dreams are like a bird that mocks,
  Flirting the feathers of his tail.
When you seize at the salt-box
  Over the hedge you'll see him sail.
Old birds are neither caught with salt nor chaff:
They watch you from the apple bough and laugh.

Poet, never chase the dream.
  Laugh yourself and turn away.
Mask your hunger, let it seem
  Small matter if he come or stay;
But when he nestles in your hand at last
Close up your fingers tight and hold him fast.

From **The Garden of the Prophet** *by* Kahlil Gibran

And he spoke to the people, his friends and his neighbours, and there was joy in their hearts and upon their eyelids.

And he said: 'You grow in sleep, and live your fuller life in your dreaming. For all your days are spent in thanksgiving for that which you have received in the stillness of the night.

'Oftentimes you think and speak of night as the season of rest, yet in truth night is the season of seeking and finding.

'The day gives unto you the power of knowledge and teaches your fingers to become versed in the art of receiving; but it is night that leads you to the treasure-house of Life.

'The sun teaches to all things that grow their longing for the light. But it is night that raises them to the stars.'

From **Poems** *by* Dorothea Eastwood

SLEEPING CHILD

Here lie all dreams, all dreams,
Hidden within his eyes.
Here rest all lovely thoughts
Secure from man's surprise.

Here float and break bright seas
Of unimpaired delight,
For though his lids are closed
He has the heart's sight.

Elders may never know
What visions haunt this head,
For from their rigid minds
Such dreams were long since fled.

Only as dark draws on
And they stand looking down,
Longed for are nights when they
Under such seas would drown.

From **The Garden of the Prophet** *by* Kahlil Gibran

And One Said: speak to us of that which is moving in your own heart even now.

And he looked upon that one, and there was in his voice a sound like a star singing, and he said: 'In your waking dream, when you are hushed and listening to your deeper self, your thoughts, like snow-flakes, fall and flutter and garment all the sounds of your spaces with white silence.

'And what are waking dreams but clouds that bud and blossom on the sky-tree of your heart? And what are your thoughts but the petals which the winds of your heart scatter upon the hills and its fields?

'And even as you wait for peace until the formless within you takes form, so shall the cloud gather and drift until the Blessed Fingers shape its grey desire to little crystal suns and moons and stars.'

From **The Collected Poems of Edward Thomas**

SNOW

In the gloom of whiteness,
In the great silence of snow,
A child was sighing
And bitterly saying 'Oh,
They have killed the white bird up there on her nest.
And down is fluttering from her breast.'
And still it fell through that dusky brightness
On the child crying for the bird in the snow.

By Arthur William Edgar O'Shaughnessy, *quoted in* **Other Men's Flowers** by Lord Wavell

ODE

We are the music-makers.
And we are the dreamers of dreams
Wandering by lone sea-breakers
And sitting by desolate streams,
  World-losers and world forsakers
On whom the pale moon gleams.
Yet we are the movers and shakers
Of the world forever, it seems.

With wonderful deathless ditties
We build up the world's great cities,
  And out of a fabulous story
  We fashion an empire's glory:
One man with a dream, at pleasure,
  Shall go forth and conquer a crown;
And three with a new song's measure
  Can trample an empire down.

We in the ages lying
  In the buried past of the earth,
Built Nineveh with our sighing,
  And Babel itself with our mirth;
And o'erthrew them with prophesying
  To the old of the new world's worth;
For each age is a dream that is dying,
  Or one that is coming to birth.

From **The White Witch** *by* Elizabeth Goudge

The vast dome of the sky arched from horizon to horizon over the heathland would have been terrifying but for the moonlight which rained down with such gentleness upon the flatness of the crouching earth. The beauty that emerged from the flatness her plum tree set with stars, the shapes of distant woods, the tower of the Church rising from the churchyard yews and the faint glow of flame from the camp-fire down in the dingle seemed to her to have been drawn upwards by the moonlight as flowers are by the sun. But sun-light can tarnish, while the beneficence gave to all it shone upon a quality of unchangeableness. The plum tree in bright sunshine was of the earth, but in the moonlight its ebony and silver had an immortal look as though it were not a tree but a spirit. She had been told that to the blind moonlight has sound, and shutting her eyes for a moment she wondered what that sound could be. Music, brought down from the stars? A choir of far-away voices, like friends greeting each other in another world? Or a murmuring of re-assurance like the wind before the dawn? Something like that, some visitation of eternity giving a meaning to the flux of things.

From **The Collected Poems** *by* Walter de la Mare

SILVER

Slowly, silently, now the moon
Walks the night in her silver shoon;
This way, and that, she peers, and sees
Silver fruit upon silver trees;
One by one the casements catch
Her beams beneath the silvery thatch;
Couched in his kennel, like a log,
With paws of silver sleeps the dog;
From their shadowy cote the white breasts peep
Of doves in a silver-feathered sleep;
A harvest mouse goes scampering by,
With silver claws, and silver eye;
And moveless fish in the water gleam,
By silver reeds in a silver stream.

From **Poems** *by* Dorothea Eastwood

CLOUDS

See how those clouds, with tips of ostrich plume,
Lean down to fan the sun before he goes,
And how he rests delighted on the hill,
To watch the feathers quiver, gold and rose.

But now his time has come and he must plunge
To empty-skied Antipodes while soon
The clouds will change their fans to pearl and white
With silver fringes to enchant the Moon.

From **Consequently I Rejoice** *by* Elizabeth Jennings

LET THERE BE

Let there be dark for us to contemplate.
Light draws the senses. O that seize of stars
Or even ember-comfort in a grate—

These blind us. Christ, teach us the *Book of Hours*
Which says 'Be silent' as we turn the page
And let the vigil come. Light overpowers.

Give us the night, the lonely privilege
Of offering our praise, a plea within
Enormous spaces lasting to the edge.

Of almost dawn, and let the birds begin
To chip at sounds, set fire to tree and hedge.

DYING

'Death cannot kill what never dies'

From **Fruits of Solitude** *by* William Penn

THE COMFORT OF FRIENDS

They that love beyond the world cannot be separated by it. Death cannot kill what never dies, nor can spirits ever be divided that love and live in the same divine principle, the root and record of their friendship.

If absence be not death, neither is theirs. Death is but crossing the world, as friends do the seas; they live in one another still.

For they must needs be present that love and live in that which is omnipresent.

In this divine glass they see face to face, and their converse is free as well as pure.

This is the comfort of friends, that though they may be said to die, yet their friendship and society are in the best sense ever present because immortal.

From the **Confessions** *of* St Augustine

Hence proceeds that grief, if a friend chance to die, and that darkness of sorrow; the heart being steeped in tears, the sweet being all turned to bitterness. Hence groweth too the death of such as live, by losing out of their lives those who die.

Blessed is the man that loves thee, and his friend in thee, and his enemy for thee. For he alone never loseth a dear friend, to whom all men are dear for his sake who is never lost.

Prayer

O God, forasmuch as earthly love is but the image of thine own eternal charity, be gracious unto those who have blessed us with their love. Do thou reward them with the abundant riches of thy grace that the love which is begun on earth may be perfected in the glory of thine own revelation from whom all true love comes and in whom it shall be consummated. Amen.

From **Towards Democracy** *by* Edward Carpenter

UNDERNEATH AND AFTER ALL

There is no peace except where I am, saith the Lord.

Though you have health—that which is called health—yet without me it is only fair covering of disease;

Though you have love, yet if I be not between and around the lovers, is their love only torment and unrest;

Though you have wealth and friends and home—all these shall come and go—there is nothing stable or secure, which shall not be taken away;

But I alone remain—I do not change.

As space spreads everywhere, and all things move and change within it, but it moves not nor changes,

So I am the space within the soul, of which the space without is but the similitude and mental image;

Comest thou to inhabit me, thou hast the entrance to all life—death shall no longer divide thee from whom thou lovest.

I am the sun that shines upon all creatures from within—gazest thou upon me thou shalt be filled with joy eternal.

Be not deceived. Soon this outer world shall drop off—thou shalt slough it away as a man sloughs his mortal body.

Learn even now to spread thy wings in that other world—the world of Equality—to swim in the ocean, my child, of Me and My love.

(Ah! have I not taught thee by the semblances of this outer world, by its alienations and deaths and mortal sufferings—all for this? For joy, ah! joy unutterable!)

From **What Is Dying?** *by* Bishop Brent

What is dying?

I am standing on the sea shore,

a ship sails to the morning breeze and starts for the ocean. She is an object of beauty and I stand watching her till at last she fades on the horizon, and someone at my side says,

'She is gone.'

Gone! Where? Gone from my sight—that is all; she is just as large in the mast's hull and spars as she was when I saw her, and just as able to bear her load of living freight to its destination.

The diminished size and total loss of sight is in me, not in her; and just at the moment when someone at my side says

'she is gone',

there are others who are watching her coming, and other voices take up a glad shout—

'There she comes'—

and that is dying.

From **Holy Sonnets** *by* John Donne

Death be not proud, though some have called thee
Mighty and dreadfull, for, thou art not soe,
For, those, whom thou think'st, thou dost overthrow,
Die not, poore death, nor yet canst thou kill mee.
From rest and sleepe, which but thy pictures bee,
Much pleasure, then from thee, much more must flow,
And soonest our best men with thee doe goe,
Rest of their bones, and soules deliverie.
Thou art slave to Fate, Chance, kings, and desperate men,
And dost with poyson, warre, and sicknesse dwell,
And poppie, or charmes can make us sleepe as well,
And better than thy stroake; why swell'st thou then?
One short sleepe past, wee wake eternally,
And death shall be no more; Death, thou shalt die.

From **Prayers of Grief and Glory** *by* Richard Harries

AS THE BLIND COMES DOWN

Some people feel that religion is anti-life, but properly understood there need be no antagonism between religion and life. For it is God who has made us physical beings and set us in a world which arouses and delights the senses. What we see and hear, taste, touch and smell is meant to be integrated into the life of faith.

Yet having said this a problem of some anguish remains; one which we need to have out with God. 'You have created us, O God, as physical beings in a world which gives pleasure. We rejoice in the sunlight and the shadows, the sound of waves and the smell of lilac—and then you take it all away from us. Our eyesight fades, our hearing becomes hard, our memory less good, until finally the blind comes down over the window of our mind.' And the point is that though we might be quite willing to give up the most basic pleasures like eating an ice cream or drinking a glass of cold lager on a hot day, our most profound and sustaining experiences, music, poetry, the sight of hills, friendships—all this too is taken away from us. And what, I wonder, does God reply?

Perhaps something like this: 'I take it away from you only to give you something better. All that pleases eye and ear does it not come from me? What you experience now is only a foretaste, a scent carried in the wind, an echo of an indescribable beauty. Know me and know a delight which never fades.' Yet still a nasty niggle remains, for the fact is that in practice trying to know God better seems so hard. Even the devout find it difficult on occasions to begin to pray and think it nice when they stop; worship too often seems a drag. Life around us is immediate and real. The world of colour and sound pulls. Those who try to go beyond the immediate sensation to God from whom it comes find an effort has to be made. I don't know what God might say to this, except, 'Go on trying—persevere. The end is worth it and no one can make the journey for you.'

Yet one practical point can, I think, be made. All those who have wanted to know God better seem to have felt the need for time on their own. Christ went away into lonely desert places to pray; monks have sought solitary caves.

. . . Goodness knows it's difficult to get a moment's silence in the noisy urban life of today but when we do it isn't a negative thing. It's a space cleared in the jungle of sound for awareness to grow—awareness of what is given as our senses wear away.

O God, we rejoice in this world of light and colour, shape and sound, but lead us beyond it to know you from whom all good things come.

From **The Face of the Deep** *by* Christina Rossetti

Safe where I cannot lie yet,
  Safe where I hope to lie too
Safe from the fume and the fret;
  You, and you,
Whom I never forget.

Safe from the frost and the snow,
  Safe from the storm and the sun,
Safe where the seeds wait to grow
  One by one
And to come back in blow.

From **The Inward Road and the Way Back** *by* Dorothee Soelle

Learning to die means no longer to hate or be burdened with fear. To learn to die means to be caught up in a great chorus that affirms life; that is what faith is. The more we learn to live in freedom from fear the more we learn to die in freedom from fear. The more we are united to that love with which we know ourselves to be at one, the more immortal we are. As Christians we know that death always lies behind us; it is love that lies ahead.

From **The English Poems of George Herbert**

THE FLOWER

How fresh, O Lord, how sweet and clean
Are thy returns! ev'n as the flowers in spring;
To which, besides their own demean,
The late-past frosts tributes of pleasure bring.
Grief melts away
Like snow in May,
As if there were no such cold thing.

Who would have thought my shrivel'd heart
Could have recover'd greennesse? It was gone
Quite under ground; as flowers depart
To see their mother-root, when they have blown;
Where they together
All the hard weather,
Dead to the world, keep house unknown.

These are thy wonders, Lord of power,
Killing and quick'ning, bringing down to hell
And up to heaven in an houre;
Making a chiming of a passing bell.
We say amisse.
This or that is:
Thy world is all, if we could spell.

O that I once past changing were,
Fast in thy Paradise, where no flower can wither!
Many a spring I shoot up fair,
Offring at heav'n, growing and groning thither:
Nor doth my flower
Want a spring-showre,
My sinnes and I joining together:

But while I grow in a straight line,
Still upwards bent, as if heav'n were mine own,
Thy anger comes, and I decline:
What frost to that? what pole is not the zone,
Where all things burn,
When thou dost turn,
And the least frown of thine is shown?

And now in age I bud again,
After so many deaths I live and write;
I once more smell the dew and rain,
And relish versing: O my onely light,
It cannot be
That I am he
On whom thy tempests fell all night.

These are thy wonders, Lord of Love,
To make us see we are but flowers that glide:
Which when we once can finde and prove,
Thou hast a garden for us, where to bide,
Who would be more,
Swelling through store,
Forfeit their Paradise by their pride.

From **Adonais** *by* P. B. Shelley

XXXIX

Peace, peace! he is not dead, he doth not sleep—
He hath awakened from the dream of life—

XL

He has outsoared the shadow of our night;
Envy and calumny and hate and pain,
And that unrest which men miscall delight,
Can touch him not and torture not again;
From the contagion of the world's slow stain
He is secure, and now can never mourn
A heart grown cold, a head grown gray in vain;
Nor, when the spirit's self has ceased to burn,
With sparkless ashes load an unlamented urn.

XLI

He lives, he wakes—'tis Death is dead, not he;
Mourn not for Adonais.—Thou young Dawn,
Turn all thy dew to splendour, for from thee
The spirit thou lamentest is not gone;
Ye caverns and ye forests, cease to moan!
Cease, ye faint flowers and fountains, and thou Air,

Which like a mourning veil thy scarf hadst thrown
O'er the abandoned Earth, now leave it bare
Even to the joyous stars which smile on its despair!

XLII

He is made one with Nature: there is heard
His voice in all her music, from the moan
Of thunder, to the song of night's sweet bird;
He is a presence to be felt and known
In darkness and in light, from herb and stone,
Spreading itself where'er that Power may move
Which has withdrawn his being to its own;
Which wields the world with never-wearied love,
Sustains it from beneath, and kindles it above.

By C. S. Lewis, *quoted in* **The Inklings** *by* Humphrey Carpenter

DEATH OF CHARLES WILLIAMS

My friendship is not ended, his death has had the very unexpected effect of making death itself look quite different.

I believe in the next life ten times more strongly than I did. . . . It is not blasphemous to believe that what was true of Our Lord is, in less degree, true of all who are in him.

They go away in order to be *with* us in a new way even closer than before. . . .

Williams says about the death of his wife, 'She was dead but her very death heightened that word supernatural.'

By Henry Vaughan

From THE WORLD

I saw Eternity the other night,
Like a great *Ring* of pure and endless light,
  All calm, as it was bright;
And round beneath it, Time in hours, days, years,
  Driv'n by the spheres

Like a vast shadow mov'd, In which the world
  And all her train were hurl'd.
The doting Lover in his queintest strain
  Did there Complain;
Neer him, his Lute, his fancy, and his flights,
  Wits sour delights;
With gloves, and knots the silly snares of pleasure,
  Yet his dear Treasure
All scatter'd lay, while he his eys did pour
  Upon a flow'r.

From **A Few Late Chrysanthemums** *by* John Betjeman

A CHILD ILL

Oh, little body, do not die.
  The soul looks out through wide blue eyes
So questioningly into mine,
  That my tormented soul replies.

'Oh little body, do not die.
  You hold the soul that talks to me
Although our conversation be
  As wordless as the windy sky.'

So looked my father at the last
  Right in my soul, before he died,
Though words we spoke went heedless past
  As London traffic-roar outside.

And now the same blue eyes I see
  Look through me from a little son,
So questioning, so searchingly
  That youthfulness and age are one.

My father looked at me and died
  Before my soul made full reply.
Lord, leave this other Light alight—
  Oh, little body, do not die.

From **The Canticle of the Sun,** *verse by* St Francis of Assisi

Blessed be thou, my Lord, for our sister the death of the body.
Naught that lives can escape her
Woe to those who die laden with mortal sin
Happy are they who do thy will in their hearts
The second death has no power over them.

Prayer *by* E.B.

O Lord, we praise thee for all those who have influenced our lives for good by their example, by their writings, their prayers, their gifts, their selflessness, their love.

All those we have loved and who have loved us—we thank thee O Lord for all they have meant to us, all they have given us of themselves. Help us to understand that 'death is only an horizon, the limit of our sight'.

We remember before thee those who are dying now and all those who watch with them, especially those who have never known thy love.

For thy Son our Lord Jesus Christ's sake. Amen.

From **Dust** *by* Rupert Brooke

Nor ever rest, nor ever lie
  Till, beyond thinking, out of view
One mote of all the dust that's I
  Shall meet one atom that was you.

From **A Vision of the Aquarian Age** *by* George Trevelyan

We here on earth have an urgent role to play . . . The soul after death will invariably turn back for contact with those it has loved. It can absorb knowledge from those still alive on earth. Indeed, the initial nourishment for the soul is drawn from the spiritual thoughts of those with whom it has affinities on earth, particularly when they are asleep. Today, however, when so many enter sleep at night without having developed any spiritual awareness, the crying need of the lost souls hungry for sustenance remains unanswered. Further-more, when a person bereft on earth is filled with unreasoning grief, a species of smoke-screen is created which prevents the soul in the beyond even finding its friend, much less establishing contact. Herein lies the immeasurable importance of re-evaluating our conceptions of death. For souls moving on, it is essentially a release which can be filled with joy. The substance of so many communications is that 'I am alright and very much alive and it is wonderful over here.'

As for the sorrow of those of us who are left behind, we must be honest and acknowledge that it is sorrow largely for ourselves—a form of self-pity. Obviously we cannot belittle the pain of parting and the accompanying sense of loss. But we must accept the basic fact of telepathic contact. The higher world is a thought world. Those residing in it are free to move with immense rapidity, and souls can blend with each other sharing consciousness. As a result, our thoughts, prayers and love for a departed friend are instantly received. Even though most of us cannot register this, we can nevertheless act on it. We should talk to our friends or relatives, bring them actively into our lives and plans, mentally discuss things with them. And we should support them with love and joy and courage as they explore ahead. Such an attitude preserves and validates our bond with the dead, but does not shackle them to earth in the wrong way. On the contrary, it is rather our unreasoning and persisting grief that binds and hurts, and in fact hinders the soul's forward progress.

Prayer *by* Henry Scott Holland

Death is nothing at all, I have only slipped away into the next room.

I am I and you are you, whatever we were to each other we are still.

Call me by my old familiar name, speak to me in the easy way which we always used.

Put no difference into your tone; wear no forced air of solemnity or sorrow.

Laugh, as we always laughed at the little jokes together.

Pray, smile, think of me, pray for me.

Let my name be ever the household word that it always was, let it be spoken without an effort, without trace of a shadow in it.

Life means all that it ever meant, it is the same as it ever was; there is absolutely unbroken continuity.

What is this death but a negligible accident? Why should I be out of mind because I am out of sight? I am but waiting for you, for an interval somewhere very near, just around the corner.

All is well.

Prayer

O Lord our God from whom neither life nor death can separate those who trust in thy love and whose love holds in its embrace thy Children in this world and in the next: so unite us to thyself that in fellowship with thee we may be always united to our loved ones whether here or there; give us courage, constancy and hope; through him who died and was buried and rose again for us, Jesus Christ our Lord. Amen.

From **Vale and Other Poems** *by* A. E.

GERMINAL

In ancient shadows and twilights
  Where childhood had strayed,
The world's great sorrows were born
  And its heroes were made.
In the lost boyhood of Judas
  Christ was betrayed.

From an article by Selwyn Cumnor *in* **The World Christian Digest**

YOUR BEREAVEMENT

Let us thank God for the years they were with us. For the gaiety and happiness and the companionship and love they gave us.

These are things that nothing can take away, they are ours to hold in our hearts and cherish all the days of our life.

Let us dwell on these things and not on the sadness of a temporary farewell.

From **Intimations of Christianity** *by* Simone Weil

Grief, said Plato, is the dissolution of harmony, the separation of contraries; joy is their reunion.

The crucifixion of the Christ has almost opened the door. . . . The door half-opened . . . Those who have the immense privilege of participating with their whole being in the Cross of Christ, go through that door they pass to the side where the secrets of God Himself are to be found.

But more generally, every sort of grief, and above all every sort of disaster well endured, makes the passage to the other side of that door possible, makes the true face of harmony seen.

That face which is turned toward the heights rends one of the veils which separate us from the beauty of God.

By Edmund Waller

The seas are quiet, when the winds give o're;
So calm are we, when Passions are no more:
For then we know how vain it was to boast
Of fleeting Things, so certain to be lost.
Clouds of Affection from our younger Eyes
Conceal that emptiness, which Age descries.

The Soul's dark Cottage, batter'd and decay'd,
Lets in new Light thro' chinks that time has made.
Stronger by weakness, wiser Men become
As they draw near to their Eternal home:
Leaving the Old, both Worlds at once they view,
That stand upon the Threshold of the New.

From **The City of God** *by* St Augustine

We shall rest and we shall see;
We shall see and we shall love.
We shall love and we shall praise;
Behold what will be, in the end without end;
For what is our end but to reach the Kingdom which has no end?

Index of Sources and Acknowledgements

The compiler acknowledges with gratitude the courtesy of the following companies and individuals in permitting the use of copyright material. For Bible versions, see under general heading 'Bible'. Page numbers appear in **bold** type.

A. E. (George William Russell), *The Candle of Vision*. Macmillan 1918. Used by permission of Colin Smythe Ltd and the A. E. Estate. **150**
———, *Collected Poems*. Macmillan 1913. Used by permission of Colin Smythe Ltd and the A. E. Estate. **34**
———, *Vale and Other Poems*. Macmillan 1931. Used by permission of Colin Smythe Ltd and the A. E. Estate. **167**
Allchin, A. M., 'Solitude and Communion in the Life of Thomas Merton' in *Christian*, Whitsun 1974. **24**
Andrew, Father, *A Gift of Light: A Collection of Thoughts*, selected and edited by Harry Griffith. Mowbray 1972. **27, 29, 46, 55**
Anonymous. **45** (epigraph), **93, 120, 122, 125, 137** (epigraph)
Anonymous, 'Prayer'. **58, 59, 82, 157, 167**
Anonymous, probably Japanese. **23**
Anonymous, Chinese proverb. **46**
Anonymous, Jewish proverb. **54**
Anonymous, heard on the radio. **94**
Anonymous, Prayer from All Saints' Church, Margaret Street, London. **30**
Anonymous, 'The Farmer's Prayer'. **60**
Anonymous, Prayer from St Mary's Abbey, West Malling, Kent. **146**
Anonymous, 'A Seventeenth-Century Nun's Prayer'. **146**
Anonymous, from *The Book of Zohar*. **54**
Anonymous, set to music by Robert Jones in *The Muse's Garden of Delight*, 1610. **71**
Anonymous, from the Parish Magazine of All Saints', Worlingham, Suffolk. **83**
Anonymous, 'Love Divine All Loves Excelling', no. 437 in *The English Hymnal*. **29**
Anonymous, quoted by St Thomas Aquinas in *Catena Aurea*. **4**
Appleton, George, 'Hopeless Situations?', *The Daily Telegraph*, 10 March 1979. Used by kind permission of *The Daily Telegraph*. **137**

——, *The Practice of Prayer*. Mowbray 1979. **140, 147**
Aubert, Edward, 'The Dynamics of Repentance', leaflet published by The Dorothy Kerin Trust n.d. **58**
Auden, W. H., *Collected Poems*. Faber 1963. Reprinted by permission of Faber & Faber Ltd. **42, 70**
——, *The Dyer's Hand*. Faber 1962. Reprinted by permission of Faber & Faber Ltd. **79**
Augustine, Saint, *Confessions*, translated by E. J. Sheed. Fontana Books 1963. **11, 47, 156**
——, *The City of God*, translated by J. W. C. Wand. Oxford University Press 1963. **169**

Bacon, Francis, 'Of Gardens', Essay XLVI, in *The Oxford Book of English Prose*, edited by Sir Arthur Quiller-Couch. Clarendon Press 1973. **8**
Baker, John Austin, *The Foolishness of God*. Darton, Longman & Todd 1970. **142**
Barkway, Lumsden, 'Introduction' to *An Anthology of the Love of God* by Evelyn Underhill (q.v.). **64**
Basset, Elizabeth, 'Longing and Listening' BBC Radio 'Epilogue', 24 June 1979. **32, 67, 93**
——, written for this volume, 1981. **23, 31, 48, 89, 165**
Beckmann, Max, 'On My Painting' in *Modern Artists on Art*, edited by Robert L. Herbert. © 1964 by Prentice-Hall, Inc. Published by Prentice-Hall, Inc., Englewood Cliffs, New Jersey 07632. **98**
Beethoven, Ludwig van, quoted in *The Life of Beethoven* by Alexander Wheelock Thayer, Princeton University Press © 1964. Published by Princeton University Press, Princeton, N.J. **121**
Benson, E. F., *Queen Lucia*. Hutchinson 1920. **81**
Berger, Peter L., *A Rumour of Angels*, p. 119. Allen Lane/Penguin 1970. Copyright © Peter L. Berger 1969. Reprinted by permission of Penguin Books Ltd. **18**
Bessiere, Gerard, *Jesus Ahead*. Burns & Oates 1975. **21, 91, 94**
Betjeman, John, 'Foreword' *A Nip in the Air*. John Murray (Publishers) Ltd 1974. **140**
——, *A Few Late Chrysanthemums*. John Murray (Publishers) Ltd 1954. **164**
Bible: The Authorized Version. Extracts from the Authorized King James Version of the Bible and the Book of Common Prayer of 1662, which are Crown Copyright, are reproduced by permission. **34, 40, 144**
Bible: The Common Bible, derived from the Revised Standard Version. Collins 1952. © 1973 by the Division of Christian Education of the National Council of the Churches of Christ in the United States of America. **3, 137, 149**
Bible: The Jerusalem Bible, published and copyright © 1966, 1967 and

1968 by Darton, Longman & Todd Ltd and Doubleday & Co. Inc. Used by permission of the publishers. **4**
Bible: *The New Testament in Modern English*, translated by J. B. Phillips. Collins 1960. **47**
Binyon, Laurence, *London Visions*. Sidgwick & Jackson 1898. **108**
Blackburn, Thomas, *Bread For the Winter Birds*. Hutchinson 1980. **24**
———, 'Station of the Globe'. **67**
Blake, Naomi, essay written for this volume, 1981. **40**
Blake, William, *Songs of Innocence* in *The Oxford Book of English Verse*, edited by Helen Gardner. Clarendon Press 1972. **79**
Blakelock, Denys, prayer printed on the Catholic Stage Guild's membership card. **143**
Blanch, Stuart, *For All Mankind*. Bible Reading Fellowship 1976. **3**
Blue, Lionel, 'Humour in Religion' in *Contact* no. 71, 1981–2. **78**
Bonhoeffer, Dietrich. Source unknown. **5**
Born, Anne, 'Dry Stone Walls' in *The Countryman* 1979. **114**
Boros, Ladislaus, *The Cosmic Christ*. Search Press 1975. **64**
———, *The Moment of Truth*. Burns & Oates 1965. **68, 71, 126**
Boston, Richard, *An Anatomy of Laughter*. Collins 1974. **78**
Brent, Bishop, 'What Is Dying?'. **158**
Brooke, Rupert, *Collected Poems*. Sidgwick & Jackson 1918. **165**
Brown, T. E., quoted in *A Vision of the Aquarian Age* by George Trevelyan (q.v.). **97**
Browning, Robert, *Summum Bonum (Asolando)* 1889. **67**
Buber, Martin, *Between Man and Man*. Routledge & Kegan Paul 1961. **59**
Burns, Robert, 'The Winter'. Words as set to music by Benjamin Britten. **68**

Cameron, Clare, 'The White Snow of Meditation', with acknowledgement to Chu Chan, in *The Science of Thought Review*, Bosham House, Chichester, Sussex PO18 8PJ. **96**
Carpenter, Edward, *Towards Democracy*. Allen & Unwin 1883. **v, 89, 124, 157**
Carruth, W. H., *Each In His Own Tongue and Other Poems*. New York, G. P. Putnam & Sons, 1908. **33**
Casals, Pablo, *Joys and Sorrows: Reflections*, as told to Albert E. Kahn. Macdonald Futura 1970. Copyright © 1970 by Albert E. Kahn. Reprinted by permission of Simon & Schuster, A Division of Gulf & Western Corporation. **12**
Casteel, John, *Rediscovering Prayer*. Hodder & Stoughton 1955. **38**
Chesterton, G. K., *The Ballad of St Barbara and Other Poems*. Methuen 1922. Used by permission of Miss D. E. Collins. **113**
Churchill, Winston, *Painting As a Pastime*. New York, Simon & Schuster. **98**
Cornford, Frances, *Collected Poems*. Cresset Press 1954. **106**
Cumnor, Selwyn, 'Your Bereavement' in *The World Christian Digest*. **168**

Curling, Claude, lecture given at the University of Geneva, April 1981, as part of a Teilhard de Chardin Centenary Conference. **24**

The Daily Office © The Joint Liturgical Group. Reproduced by permission of S.P.C.K. and the Epworth Press. **100**

Davies, Gary, article in the *Clarion*, parish magazine for St Mary The Boltons, London. **58, 148**

de la Mare, Walter, *The Complete Poems*. Faber 1954. Used by permission of The Literary Trustees of Walter de la Mare and The Society of Authors as their representative. **9, 76, 116, 125, 154**

de Mello, Anthony, *Sadhana: A Way to God*. Anand, Gujarat Sahitya Prakash, 1978. **141**

Dix, Gregory, *The Shape of the Liturgy*, A. & C. Black 1945. **28**

Donne, John, *Holy Sonnets* in *The Metaphysical Poets*, edited by Helen Gardner. Penguin 1957. **158**

Eastwood, Dorothea, *Poems*. Privately printed 1963. **130, 152, 155**

Ecclestone, Alan, *The Night Sky of the Lord*. Darton, Longman & Todd 1980. **96**

———, *Yes To God*. Darton, Longman & Todd 1975. **127**

Edna Mary, Sister, and Marshall, Michael, *A Pattern of Faith*. Hodder & Stoughton 1966. **38**

Einstein, Albert, *The Universe and Dr. Einstein*. New York, Lincoln Barnett. **15**

Fausset, Hugh L'Anson, *Fruits of Silence*. New York, Abelard-Schuman, 1965. **95**

Fonteyn, Margot, *The Magic of Dance*. BBC Publications 1979. **105**

Fromm, Eric, *The Art of Loving*. Allen & Unwin; New York, Harper & Row, 1957. **73**

Francis of Assisi, Saint, in *St Francis of Assisi* by Elizabeth Goudge (q.v.). **73, 121**

———, verse added to *The Canticle of the Sun*. **165**

Furlong, Monica, *God's A Good Man and Other Poems*. Mowbray 1974. **50**

———, *Travelling In*. Hodder & Stoughton 1971. © Monica Furlong 1971. **69**

Gaunt, Belle Valerie, and Trevelyan, George, *A Tent in Which to Pass a Summer's Night*. Coventure Ltd 1977. **116**

George VI, BBC Radio Broadcast, 15 August 1945. **83**

Gibran, Kahlil, *The Garden of the Prophet*. Heinemann 1934, **151, 152**

———, *Jesus, the Son of Man*. Heinemann 1927. **129**

Glubb, John, *The Fate of Empires and the Search for Survival*. Blackwood 1978. **47**

Goldwater, Robert, and Treves, Marco (eds.), *Artists on Art*. John Murray (Publishers) Ltd 1976. **102**

Goudge, Elizabeth, *The Rosemary Tree*. Hodder & Stoughton 1976. **38**
———, *St Francis of Assisi*. Duckworth 1959. **73, 121**
———, *The White Witch*. Hodder & Stoughton 1958. **74, 154**
Graham, Virginia, *Consider the Years*. Jonathan Cape 1946. Used by permission of the author and *Punch*. **85**
Graves, Robert, *Fairies and Fusiliers*. Heinemann 1917. **151**
Griffiths, Bede, *Return to the Centre*. Collins 1978. **22**
Grou, Père, in *The Practice of Prayer* by George Appleton (q.v.). **140**

Hamblin, Henry Thomas, 'Drawing Heaven Down to Earth' in *The Science of Thought Review* (*see* Cameron), May 1979. **139**
Hammarskjöld, Dag, *Markings*, translated by W. H. Auden and Leif Sjöberg. Faber 1964. Reprinted by permission of Faber & Faber Ltd. **4, 15, 21, 31, 45, 56, 60, 98, 114**
Harries, Richard, *Prayers of Grief and Glory*. Lutterworth Press 1979. **32, 77, 159**
———, *Prayers of Hope*. BBC Publications 1975. **86**
Hassall, Christopher, *Out of the Whirlwind: A Play for Westminster Abbey*. Heinemann 1953. **114**
Hazlitt, William, *Liber Amoris*. 1823. **65**
Herbert, George, *The English Poems of George Herbert*. J. M. Dent 1974. **10, 56, 111, 161**
Holland, Henry Scott, 'Prayer'. **166**
Holmes, Oliver Wendell, no. 434 in *The English Hymnal*. **16**
Hopkins, Gerard Manley, *Poems*. Oxford University Press 1967. **22**
Houselander, Caryll, *The Reed of God*. Sheed & Ward 1944. **57**
Hoyland, J. S. Source unknown. **142**
Hugo, Victor. **116** (epigraph)

Israel, Martin, *Precarious Living*. Hodder & Stoughton 1976. **93**

Janouch, Gustav, *Conversations With Kafka*, translated by Goronwy Rees. André Deutsch 1971. **46, 75, 122, 130**
Jennings, Elizabeth, *Consequently I Rejoice*. Carcanet New Press 1977. **110, 155**
John of the Cross, Saint, *The Mystical Doctrine of St John of the Cross*, translated by David Lewis. Sheed & Ward 1934. **65**
Johnson, Raynor, *A Pool of Reflections*. Hodder & Stoughton 1975. **16**
Jones, Jack Raymond, *The Man Who Loved the Sun: The Life of Vincent Van Gogh*. Evans Brothers 1966. **101**
Jones, Rufus M., *Christian Faith and Practice in the Experience of the Religious Society of Friends*, chapter 4, section 244 [1960 edition]. **26**
Jonson, Ben, 'So Sweet Is She' from *Celebration of Charis IV: Her Triumph*. **67**
Julian of Norwich, *Enfolded In Love*, translated by members of the Julian Shrine. Darton, Longman & Todd 1980. **4, 13**

———, *Revelations of Divine Love*, translated by James Walsh. Anthony Clarke Books 1973. **42**

Jung, C. G., *Psychology and Religion: East and West*, translated by R. F. C. Hull. Vol. 11 of *The Collected Works of C. G. Jung*. Princeton University Press. Copyright © 1970 by Princeton University Press. Reprinted by permission. Routledge & Kegan Paul 1970. **58**

———, *The Spirit in Man, Art, and Literature*, translated by R. F. C. Hull, Bollingen Series xx, vol. 15 of *The Collected Works of C. G. Jung*. Princeton University Press 1966. Copyright © 1966 by Princeton University Press. Reprinted by permission. Routledge & Kegan Paul 1967. **60, 99**

Kafka, Franz, in *Springs of Jewish Wisdom*. Search Press 1969. **54**

Keller, Helen, quoted in *God of a Hundred Names*. Gollancz 1962. **10**

Lawrence, D. H., *Selected Poems*, edited by Keith Sagar. Penguin 1972. **113**

Lefebvre, Georges, *Simplicity*. Darton, Longman & Todd 1975. **32**

Lewis, C. S., *A Grief Observed*. Faber 1961. Reprinted by permission of Faber & Faber Ltd. **90**

———, *Poems*. Collins 1964. **143**

———, *The Problem of Pain*. Geoffrey Bles 1940. **82**

———, in *The Inklings* by Humphrey Carpenter. Allen & Unwin 1978. **163**

Lincoln, Abraham (attributed to). Source unknown. **61**

Mace, Patrick, in 'It Won't Last For Ever But It's Not Done Yet', a dramatic verse sequence about Winchester Cathedral first performed 1940; Winchester Cathedral publication. **111**

Man, Felix H., *Eight European Artists*. Heinemann 1935. **110**

Marshall, Michael, 'Thought For the Day, BBC Radio broadcast, published in *Thought For the Day*, BBC Publications 1974, (adapted). **93**

Martin, P. W., *Experiment in Depth*. Routledge & Kegan Paul 1955. **54**

Masefield, John, *Poems*. Heinemann 1923. Reprinted by permission of The Society of Authors as the literary representative of the Estate of John Masefield and by permission of Macmillan Publishing Company. **83, 103**

May, J. Lewis, *Cardinal Newman*. Geoffrey Bles 1929. **20**

Mayne, Michael, 'Prayer For the Day', BBC Radio broadcast, 1 and 2 October 1980. **90, 91**

McGlashan, Alan, *The Savage and Beautiful Country*. Chatto & Windus 1966. **18**

Menuhin, Yehudi. Used by permission of the author. **121**

Merton, Thomas, *The Sign of Jonas*. Sheldon Press 1976. **10**

Millay, Edna St Vincent, *Collected Poems*. New York, Harper & Row. Copyright 1917, 1945 by Edna St Vincent Millay. **6**

Millet, Jean-Francois, letter to Theophile Thore in *Artists on Art* (*see* Goldwater, Robert, and Treves, Marco). **102**

Moore, Henry, in *Eight European Artists* by Felix H. Man (q.v.). **110**

Muir, Edwin, *The Collected Poems of Edwin Muir*, edited by T. S. Eliot. Faber 1964. Reprinted by permission of Faber & Faber Ltd. **94**

Neruda, Pablo, verse quoted in *Jesus Ahead* by Gerard Bessiere (q.v.). **91**

Niebuhr, Reinhold. Prayer quoted by George Appleton (q.v.). **137**

Ó hUiggin, Tadhg Óg, in *A Celtic Miscellany* by Kenneth H. Jackson. Routledge & Kegan Paul, 1951. **9**

O'Shaughnessy, Arthur William Edgar, in *Other Men's Flowers* by Lord Wavell. Jonathan Cape 1944. **153**

Parker–Rhodes, Damaris, 'Truth: A Path and Not a Possession', Swarthmore Lecture 1977. **20, 145**

Pascal, Blaise, in *Springs of Consolation*. Search Press 1968. **53**

Paul, Jean, in *Springs of Consolation*. Search Press 1968. **33**

Peake, Mervyn, *Selected Poems*. Faber 1972. **14, 37, 112**

Peers, E. Allison, *Songs of the Lover and the Beloved*. S.P.C.K. 1931. **39**

Penn, William, *Christian Faith and Practice* (*see* Jones, Rufus M.), section 460 (1726). **144**

———, *Some Fruits of Solitude*. 1693. **156**

Pettit, C. I., *A One-Hour Service for Good Friday*. S.P.C.K. 1973. **52**

Philaret of Moscow, Metropolitan, quoted in *The Orthodox Way* by Kallistos Ware (q.v.). **3**

Plato. **15** (epigraph)

Plunkett, Joseph, quoted in *A Tent in Which to Pass a Summer's Night* (*see* Gaunt, Belle Valerie, and Trevelyan, George). **11**

Priestland, Gerald, 'To What Can We Witness Together?' in *Common Ground*, no. 1, 1981. **13**

Queneau, Raymond, quoted in *Jesus Ahead* by Gerard Bessiere (q.v.). **21**

Raine, Kathleen, *Collected Poems of Kathleen Raine*. Allen & Unwin 1981. **72, 133**

Ratiner, Steven, 'Human Bridges' published as 'Embracing the Bridge Idea' in *The Christian Science Monitor*, 15 September 1980. © 1980 Steven Ratiner. All rights reserved. Used with permission. **101**

Revelation: Letters written from the Other Side of Death. Edgar G. Dunstan & Co. 1926. **100, 118**

Rhymes, Douglas A., *Through Prayer to Reality*, pages 46–7. Copyrighted 1974 by The Upper Room, 1908 Grand Avenue, Nashville, Tenn. 37202. Used by permission of the publisher. **34**

Riley, Katie, in 'Katie's Prayer' by Pleasaunce Holtum. *Quaker Monthly*, April 1981. (Not originally written for publication and discovered by accident by Pleasaunce Holtum.) **62**

Rilke, Rainer Maria, *Later Poems*, translated by J. B. Leishman. Hogarth Press. Used by permission of St John's College, Oxford, and The Hogarth Press Ltd. **127**

———, Source unknown. **64**

Roberts, Peter, 'Prayer' in *The Science of Thought Review* (*see* Cameron), April 1979. **138**

Rolle, Richard. **64** (epigraph)

Rossetti, Christina, *Collected Poems*. Macmillan 1904. **160**

Russell, Bertrand, in *Springs of Consolation*. Search Press 1968. **37**

Sackville-West, Victoria, *The Garden*. Michael Joseph 1946. Reprinted by permission of Curtis Brown Ltd, London, on behalf of The Estate of Victoria Sackville-West. **21**

Salinas, Pedro, quoted in *Jesus Ahead* by Gerard Bessiere (q.v.). **94**

Sandburg, Carl, 'Tentative (First Model) Definitions of Poetry'. New York, Harcourt, Brace Jovanovich, 1928. Copyright © 1928 Carl Sandburg. **128**

Sassoon, Siegfried, *Siegfried's Journey*. Faber 1945. Reprinted by permission of Faber and Faber Ltd. **120**

Shaffer, Peter, *Equus*. Samuel French 1973. **19**

Shakespeare, William, *Sonnets*. **69**

Shelley, P. B., 'A Defence of Poetry'. 1840. **124**

———, *Adonais* and *Prometheus Unbound* in *Poetical Works*. Oxford University Press 1978. **7, 21, 25, 149, 162**

Silver, Daphne, *No Memory of Crying*. Privately printed 1980. **76, 104**

Smith, Stevie, *The Collected Poems of Stevie Smith*. Allen Lane 1975. Used by permission of James MacGibbon, executor. **70, 92**

Soelle, Dorothee, *The Inward Road and the Way Back*. Darton, Longman & Todd 1978. **36, 56, 149, 160**

Solzhenitsyn, Alexander, 'One Word of Truth', Nobel Prize speech. The Bodley Head 1970. **128, 131**

Stark, Freya, *Peak in Darien*. John Murray (Publishers) Ltd 1976. **52**

———, *Perseus in the Wind*. John Murray (Publishers) Ltd 1948. **26, 62**

———, *The Zodiac Arch*. John Murray (Publishers) Ltd 1968. **25, 51**

Stone, Irving, *The Agony and the Ecstasy*. Collins 1961. **109**

———, (ed.), *Dear Theo: An Autobiography of Vincent Van Gogh From His Letters*. Constable 1937. **101**

Stuart, Eve, *Sheet-Anchor*. Sidgwick & Jackson 1944. **74**

Symeon, Saint, *Hymns of Divine Love*, translated by G. A. Maloney, S.J. Denville, New Jersey, Dimension Books. **17**

Tagore, Rabindranath, *Creative Unity*. Macmillan 1922. By permission of

the Trustees of the Tagore Estate and Macmillan, London and Basingstoke. **82**
———, *Fruit Gathering.* Macmillan 1916. By permission of the Trustees of the Tagore Estate and Macmillan, London and Basingstoke. **51**
———, *Gitanjali.* Macmillan 1913. By permission of the Trustees of the Tagore Estate and Macmillan, London and Basingstoke. **6, 86, 104, 126**
———, (tr.), *One Hundred Poems of Kabir.* Macmillan 1915. By permission of the Trustees of the Tagore Estate and Macmillan, London and Basingstoke. **108**
———, (tr.). *Sadhana.* Macmillan 1913. By permission of the Trustees of the Tagore Estate and Macmillan, London and Basingstoke. **66**
Taylor, John V., *The Go-Between God.* S.C.M. Press 1972. **19, 20, 92, 93**
Thomas, Edward, *Collected Poems of Edward Thomas*, edited by R. George Thomas. Oxford University Press 1978. **153**
Thomas, R. S., *Selected Poems (Tares).* Hart-Davis 1961. Used by permission of Granada Publishing Ltd. **117**
———, *Selected Poems 1946–68.* Hart-Davis 1973. **144**
Traherne, Thomas, *Poems of Felicity.* **35, 75**
Trevelyan, George, *A Vision of the Aquarian Age.* Coventure Ltd 1977. **48, 51, 165**
Trine, Ralph Waldo, *In Tune With the Infinite.* Bell 1900. **22**

Underhill, Evelyn, *An Anthology of the Love of God.* Mowbray 1953. **50**
———, *Theophanies.* J. M. Dent 1916. Copyright © 1926 by Evelyn Underhill. **149**

Vanda, Poppea, in *The Sleeping Ballerina* by Anton Dolin. Frederick Muller 1966. **103**
van der Looy, H., *Rule for a New Brother*, translated by the Benedictine nuns of Cockfosters. Darton, Longman & Todd 1973. **137**
van der Post, Laurens, *A Mantis Carol.* Hogarth Press 1975. Used by permission of the author and The Hogarth Press Ltd. **106**
———, *Venture to the Interior.* Hogarth Press 1952. Used by permission of the author and The Hogarth Press Ltd. **45**
Vanstone, W. H., *Love's Endeavour, Love's Expense.* Darton, Longman & Todd 1977. **6, 53, 66**
Vaughan, Henry, in *The Metaphysical Poets*, edited by Helen Gardner. Penguin 1957. **163**

Waller, Edmund, in *The Metaphysical Poets*, edited by Helen Gardner. Penguin 1957. **168**
Ware, Kallistos, *The Orthodox Way.* Mowbray 1979. **3, 17**
Weil, Simone, *Intimations of Christianity.* Routledge & Kegan Paul 1957. **12, 118, 168**
Whistler, Laurence, *The Initials in the Heart.* Hart-Davis 1964. **17, 78**

White, Patrick, from the fly-leaf of *The Solid Mandala*. Jonathan Cape 1976. **91**
Whiting, Lilian, *The Life Radiant*. Gay & Bird 1905. **60**
Williams, H. A., *Becoming What I Am*. Darton, Longman & Todd 1977. **17**
——, *Tensions*. Mitchell Beazley 1972. **80**

The compiler and publishers of this book have made every endeavour to trace the copyright owners of each extract. There do, however, remain a small number of short extracts for which the source is unknown to the compiler and publisher. The publisher would be glad to hear from the copyright owners of these extracts and due acknowledgement will be made in all future editions of the book.